Presented to

_____

by

_____

On the Occasion of

_____

Date

_____

(SECRETS OF)

B*e*AUTY

A 60-DAY DEVOTIONAL FOR THE INNER YOU

MICHELLE MEDLOCK ADAMS

BARBOUR
PUBLISHING

Published by Barbour Publishing, Inc., P.O. Box 719, Uhrichsville, Ohio 44683, www.barbourbooks.com

Our mission is to publish and distribute inspirational products offering exceptional value and biblical encouragement to the masses.

Member of the
Evangelical Christian
Publishers Association

Printed in the United States of America.
5 4 3 2 1

"The LORD does not look at the things man looks at.
Man looks at the outward appearance,
but the LORD looks at the heart."

1 SAMUEL 16:7 NIV

For my mother, Marion,
the most beautiful woman I know.
Love you!

Contents

A BEAUTIFUL AROMA

In fact, God thinks of us as a perfume
that brings Christ to everyone.
For people who are being saved,
this perfume has a sweet smell
and leads them to a better life.

2 CORINTHIANS 2:15–16 CEV

She breezed in and sat down in front of me at an Indiana University basketball game on that cold February night. She was an older woman, dressed in a navy business suit, with a red and white scarf tied stylishly around her neck. Her silver hair was neatly tucked behind her ears in a classic bob, and her lipstick was a perfect IU crimson color.

I would have guessed her to be in her early fifties—probably an IU professor. As she settled into her seat, a wonderful aroma filled the air. It broke through the smells of stale popcorn and overcooked hot dogs and filled my nostrils. I inhaled deeply and said, "Mmmm."

"Do you smell that?" I whispered to my mother.

"Yes, it's marvelous," she answered.

There was no doubt. The wonderful aroma had wafted in with the classy lady in front of us. As the halftime buzzer sounded, I leaned forward and tapped the woman on her shoulder.

"Excuse me, ma'am. You smell so wonderful. Could you tell me what you're wearing?"

"Thank you," she said, then told me the name of her perfume.

I shared the information with my mother,

and we each made a mental note about our next perfume purchase. I wanted to smell just like the classy lady with the silver hair.

You know, the Bible says we are the aroma of Christ. When we enter a room, we should carry His fragrance with us. His aroma should be so pleasing on us that people will tap us on the shoulder and ask, "Excuse me, ma'am. You smell wonderful. What are you wearing?" With that opening, we can share Jesus Christ with every person who notices our Christlike aroma.

Maybe your fragrance smells more like those overcooked weenies or stale popcorn. If so, you just need a "smell makeover." Ask God to replace your human smell with His divine fragrance so that you will be a witness of His sweetness everywhere you go. Ask the Lord to fill you with His fragrant love so that it enters the room even before you do. He will. He doesn't want His children to go around smelling stinky. After all, we are the aroma of Christ, and that's better than the finest perfume.

THE MOST BEAUTIFUL WOMAN IN THE WORLD. . .

They saw that his face was radiant.
Then Moses would put the veil back over
his face until he went in to speak with the
LORD.

EXODUS 34:35 NIV

Film legend Audrey Hepburn was named the most naturally beautiful woman of all time by a panel of experts in June 2004. Hepburn, the star of *Roman Holiday* and *Breakfast at Tiffany's*, topped the poll of beauty editors, makeup artists, fashion editors, model agencies, and fashion photographers who were asked to choose their top ten beauties from the list of one hundred compiled on www.smh.com. The women were chosen for their "embodiment of natural beauty, healthy living, *beautiful on the inside and out*, with great skin and a natural glow to their personality, as well as their complexion."

The article went on to say that Audrey Hepburn is the personification of natural beauty because "she has a rare charm and *inner beauty* that radiates when she smiles. Her skin looks fresh in all her films and her personality really shines through as someone warm and lively."

Wow, that's quite a tribute, huh? Wouldn't it be great to make the Top 100 Beautiful Women of All Time list—let alone be voted number one? But did you notice that Audrey Hepburn's inner beauty was mentioned twice in the judges' reasoning for choosing her? Sure, there were many other beauties that made the list—Marilyn

Monroe, Cleopatra, et cetera. Some may have been even more beautiful than Hepburn, but apparently their inner beauty was found lacking, even though their exterior beauty was striking.

That's good news, isn't it? That means even if our skin isn't flawless, even if our teeth aren't perfectly straight, and even if our hair has more bad days than good ones, we can still "radiate beauty" because of our gorgeous inner looks. In other words, if your heart is filled with the love of Jesus, that is going to cause you to glow. Did you know that Moses had to cover his face after he had spent time in God's presence because his face actually glowed? It's true!

Spend some time with God today, and get a makeover by the Master. Soon, you'll radiate His love, and people will find you attractive. You might even say, "You'll glow, girl!"

A Weighty Issue

*"If any of you lacks wisdom,
he should ask God, who gives
generously to all without finding
fault, and it will be given to him."*

James 1:5 NIV

S tanding in line at the supermarket, you can't help noticing the various women's magazines with headlines such as: LOSE 10 POUNDS IN 10 DAYS! WALK YOUR WAY TO A HEALTHY WEIGHT! LOSE THOSE LAST FIVE POUNDS EATING TOFU! And if you're like me, you probably buy several of those magazines each month and try eating tofu for a few days until you give in and have a package of M&Ms.

With each decade, managing your weight becomes more difficult. Our metabolisms slow down if we're not working out regularly, and the weight slowly acquires on our midsections, hips, and thighs. Ugh!

If your "fat jeans" fit perfectly today, then you're not alone. According to the American Obesity Organization, more than half of adult U.S. women are overweight, and more than one-third are obese. Obviously, we have some work to do in this area. But here's the good news: We don't have to do that work alone.

God cares about every little thing that affects our lives—including those extra five, ten, or twenty pounds that are hanging on for dear life! Let Him help you to achieve your ideal weight.

Ask Him to get involved in your quest for fitness and a healthy lifestyle.

My pastor's wife had struggled with her weight off and on for years, and then she finally got a plan. No, it wasn't Weight Watchers, LA Weight Loss, or Jenny Craig. It was God's plan! She said that she prayed about her weight issue, and God impressed upon her to do three things: Drink more water than soft drinks; quit eating after 6:00 p.m.; and walk two miles three days a week. Those instructions didn't seem that hard, so she started following them. Twenty pounds lighter now, she is a happier, healthier woman.

The plan God gave my pastor's wife may not be a perfect plan for you, but rest assured, God has a weight-loss plan with your name on it. Just ask for His wisdom today, and leave those supermarket magazines on the racks. Who likes tofu, anyway?

WALKING WITH THE LORD

Let us not become vainglorious.

GALATIANS 5:26 ASV

In my teens and twenties, looking good was always an issue. I exercised not because I wanted to be healthier. No, I exercised so that my Levi's would fit better. I exercised so that I could strut my stuff in a two-piece bathing suit. I exercised so that I could wear the latest, hip fashions and look good.

Now that I'm in my midthirties, I still want to look good, but I am more conscious about being fit. When I hit the treadmill, it's not just so I can burn those Snickers' calories from earlier. No, now I am exercising so that I can still be around when my daughters have children. Now I exercise so that I can enjoy those golden years with my husband. Now I exercise so I can be a healthy vessel the Lord can use.

And guess what? Exercising is no longer such a burden. Okay, I'll be honest. I don't love to jog. I love to *have* jogged—period. But I am enjoying the different mind-set I have as I approach exercise. Now that it's no longer all about me and it's all about my family and serving the Lord, I seem to be able to jog more minutes, log more miles, and have more joy as I do.

If you're struggling with this whole fitness thing, like I was, maybe you need to change your motives, like I did. Ask God to help you take your eyes off yourself and put them back on Him. He wants you to be healthy and fit so that He can use you and so that you can enjoy life to its fullest. When you understand that truth, it gives "Just do it" a whole new meaning, doesn't it?

Exercise is actually a gift from God. It is a God-designed activity that has many health benefits—lowering blood pressure, increasing your metabolism, counteracting depression, preventing the atrophy of your muscles, increasing flexibility, preventing osteoporosis, and many, many more. So go ahead. Get fit for all the right reasons and enjoy all the benefits. God wants to help you discover a better, healthier version of you!

HERE COMES THE JUDGE

I can do everything through him
who gives me strength.
PHILIPPIANS 4:13 NIV

Do you ever worry about what others think of you? I've found that most women struggle with this issue of being judged—even gorgeous, "got it all together" women. One of my dearest friends is absolutely beautiful. Would you believe that even she worries what others think of her? I once heard her say, "I'd love to do more teaching, but I'm just not ready."

I started thinking, *Wow, if she's not ready, nobody is ready. I've never met anyone who studies the Word of God more than she does.* So I said, "You are *so* ready. You probably have more of God's Word on the inside of you than anyone else I know." With that, she lowered her head and sighed. I had touched on something that upset her.

"What's the problem?" I pushed.

"Well, I have to lose at least fifteen more pounds before I'll be ready. I worry that everyone will be looking at how big my behind is rather than focusing on the message God's given me to speak."

I couldn't believe my ears. The devil had so deceived her. She had become so worried about what others would think of her that she wasn't walking in the fullness of God. She wasn't allowing herself to be used by Him.

As I drove home that day, I began to think back on all of the times I'd allowed my worries to keep me from serving God. I thought about specific instances when I'd been so afraid of being judged by others that I had completely missed an opportunity to serve Him. It made me sad—not just for me, but for all of my sisters in Christ who had done the same thing.

Are you one of those sisters? Have you been allowing your insecurities and fear of being judged to keep you from doing great things for God? If so, don't be sad. Just give those concerns to God and ask Him to fill you up with His love and confidence. Remind yourself throughout the day that you can do all things through Christ who gives you strength, and then go forward and change the world. You have much to offer!

WORDS OF WISDOM FROM ELEANOR ROOSEVELT

*As God's chosen people, holy and dearly loved,
clothe yourselves with compassion, kindness,
humility, gentleness and patience.*

COLOSSIANS 3:12 NIV

Eleanor Roosevelt has been called the most revered woman of her generation. She made a difference every place she ever dwelled. She not only gave birth to six children, but she also served as a dynamic political helpmate to her husband, Franklin Delano Roosevelt.

Eleanor Roosevelt literally transformed the role of First Lady, holding press conferences, traveling to all parts of the country, giving lectures and radio broadcasts, and expressing her opinions in a daily syndicated newspaper column called "My Day." You might say that she was a spitfire, a woman on a mission, a servant to humankind, a loving wife and mother, and a role model for all women.

Knowing of her accomplishments, it was very interesting to discover Mrs. Roosevelt was a very shy and awkward child. Her mother died when she was only eight years old, and her father died just two years later. It wasn't until she began attending a distinguished school in England that she began to develop self-confidence. During that self-discovery phase, she wrote, "No matter how plain a woman may be, if truth and loyalty are stamped upon her face, all will be attracted to her."

What wise words from such a young teen, huh?

If only we all understood that truth. For years, society has told us that if we're not beautiful—like the cover girls on magazines—then we have no place in this world. Many women feel they don't have a voice because they don't fit into a size 6 suit. Many of us have bought the lie. But no more! Like Eleanor Roosevelt, we, too, can overcome our shyness and change our world.

Have you ever met someone who isn't really that physically attractive, but after you're around that person for any length of time, you see her as lovely? That's the same quality Eleanor Roosevelt understood. She got it! It's not what's on the outside that makes us worthy, lovely, and attractive. That kind of beauty is fleeting. It's that loyalty, truth, and love on the inside of us, spilling out onto others, that draws people to us. In other words, it's the Jesus in us that makes us irresistible.

If you're feeling plain, unworthy, unattractive, and unnoticed—give yourself a makeover from the inside out. Ask God to develop the fruits of the Spirit within you, and allow the Lord to fill you with His love. Pretty soon, you'll be confident and irresistible—just like Eleanor Roosevelt. And you'll make a difference every place you go!

"YOU LOOK MAHVELOUS!"

*Thank you for making me
so wonderfully complex!
Your workmanship is marvelous—
and how well I know it.*

PSALM 139:14 NLT

I have a friend named Mary whose very favorite saying is "You look mahvelous!" This gal knows how to give a compliment. No one can say it quite like Mary. You may not know Mary, but I bet you remember the character Billy Crystal made famous on *Saturday Night Live* by saying, "You look mahvelous!" (In the 1980s, he even had a song titled "You Look Mahvelous!" that played on radio across the United States.)

I've always loved that saying. It's better than just saying, "Hey, you look all right." It's much more exciting to hear, "You look mahvelous!" After fourteen years of marriage, my husband knows which answers will get him into trouble. For instance, if I ask, "Does this outfit make me look fat?" his answer had better be "No. Are you kidding? How could anything ever make you look fat?" And if I ask, "How do I look?" he'd better not say, "You look okay" or "You look fine." Why? Because *okay* and *fine* translate into *adequate* or *you'll do*. No woman wants to feel like she's just "okay." Women want to look and feel marvelous, right?

Well, in the real world, we often don't feel like we look marvelous. In fact, we may not feel like we even measure up to okay or fine. Am

I right? Maybe you were raised in a home where praise was rarely given, so you're not used to hearing compliments. Or maybe you're married to a person who doesn't know how to make you feel special with words. Or maybe you never feel like you look marvelous—no matter how many times you hear it.

I have good news for you. God thinks you're marvelous! He created you exactly how you are. So even if you hate your freckles or you wish you were taller, God thinks you're perfect. He adores you, and He wants you to find out just how much. Go to His Word and read how much He loves you. He tells you over and over again throughout the Bible. Spend some time with Him, and find out how marvelous God thinks you are today.

Put Your Smile on

A merry heart does good, like medicine.

<small>Proverbs 17:22 NKJV</small>

Ever notice that when you smile it's like an instant face-lift? Your eyes look brighter. Your cheeks appear lifted. You just look better with a grin on your face. Not only does smiling make you look better, but also it is good for you—especially when your smile is accompanied by a chuckle or two.

According to information on the Discover Health Web site, by the time a child reaches nursery school, he or she will laugh about three hundred times a day. Know how many times a day an average adult laughs?

Only *seventeen* giggles a day, and that's just not enough. We need to laugh on a regular basis, and laughter starts with a smile.

Proverbs 17:22 says, "A merry heart does good, like medicine."

In other words, laughter is good for your body. Laughter actually stimulates circulation, produces a sense of well-being, exercises the face and stomach muscles, stimulates the production of endorphins (the body's natural painkillers), and provides oxygen to the brain, to name a few benefits. Here are a few more facts to encourage your laughter:

*A few ha-ha's are good for your heart! According to a study at the University of Maryland Medical Center, laughter may actually help prevent heart disease. The study found that people with heart disease were 40 percent less likely to laugh in a variety of situations compared to people of the same age without heart disease.

*Giggling is a good workout! It has been proven that hearty laughter actually burns calories—as many as equivalent to several minutes on a rowing machine or an exercise bike. Now which would you rather do? Work out on a rowing machine or laugh awhile?

*Laughter can reduce stress! Laughter eases muscle tension and psychological stress, which keeps the brain alert.

Last but not least, laughter makes you more attractive. People are naturally drawn to jolly people. Simply by wearing a smile, you become more approachable and better liked. So go ahead. Smile. Chuckle. Giggle. Give a big ol' belly laugh, as they say in Texas. It's an instant makeover, and it just might be the medicine you've needed.

Makeup—Don't Leave Home without It

*"The L*ORD *does not look at*
the things man looks at.
Man looks at the outward appearance,
*but the L*ORD *looks at the heart."*

1 SAMUEL 16:7 NIV

My pastor leaned over the pulpit, smiled, and said, "I always tell my wife to treat her makeup like the commercial says to treat your American Express card—don't leave home without it!"

I glanced over at his wife and thought, *Yep. He is so sleeping on the pastoral couch tonight.*

All teasing aside, the dog may be man's best friend, but mascara is a lady's best bud. My mama always told me to put on a little lipstick and some mascara at the very least, because you never know who you might run into at the grocery store. She's right, of course. The one time I headed to Wal-Mart without a speck of makeup on, I practically saw my entire high school graduating class. I wanted to hide in the display of toilet paper until all the lights were dimmed and I could bolt to my car. Ever been there?

Makeup is an amazing thing. It can hide blemishes. It can enhance your eyes. It can make thin lips look luscious and moist. It can transform stubby, faded eyelashes into long, curled, and dark lashes. It can give your cheeks color, making you appear well rested when you've been up all night. Makeup is a gift from God—I'm sure of it!

But wouldn't it be even better if our skin had

no flaws to cover? Wouldn't it be better if our lips were already the perfect shade of pink? Wouldn't it be better if our cheeks were naturally rosy and our lashes naturally thick? If we were already perfect, we wouldn't need anything to cover our imperfections.

Well, maybe our outsides aren't perfect, but if you've asked Jesus to be your Lord and Savior, your heart is blemish-free. See, God didn't just cover our sins with His heavenly Father foundation. Instead, He sent Jesus to die for us and take away all of our sins. Isn't that good news? The moment we asked Jesus to forgive us, we became blemish-free on the inside.

That's how God sees us—perfect and blemish-free. The Word says that God looks on the heart, while man looks on the outward appearance. So while you might want to put a little paint on the barn before venturing out, your heart is already lovely.

DRINK UP!

"Whoever believes in me,
as the Scripture has said,
streams of living water will flow
from within him."

JOHN 7:38 NIV

gua. H$_2$O. Water. You can call it
whatever you want as long as you drink
lots of it. Water is one of the best beauty
secrets in the world. Did you know that water
suppresses the appetite naturally and helps the
body metabolize stored fat? In other words, water
helps you lose weight. So drink up!

Weight loss is just one of the benefits of
drinking water. There are more reasons to drink
H$_2$O: Water carries needed nutrients through
the body and carries unwanted waste out of the
body. In other words, water helps cleanse your
body internally. Need more convincing?

Here are some additional water facts to get
you motivated.

• Water maintains blood volume and proper
muscle tone.

• Water can improve the appearance of your
skin.

• Water is a great treatment for fluid retention.

• Water keeps you from being dehydrated. (Did
you know that one of the most common reasons for
headaches and anxiety attacks is dehydration?)

Ultimately, you should drink six to eight glasses
of water every day. That's a good gauge, but here's
an even better one. Try dividing your weight in half

and drink that many ounces of water a day. That should be your goal.

Okay, now that you're convinced you should be drinking H_2O, I want to talk about another kind of water—the Living Water. If you've asked Jesus to be the Lord of your life, you're filled with the Holy Spirit, which is the Living Water. This water will make you beautiful on the inside and spiritually fit.

The Word talks of the Living Water in John 4. Remember the Samaritan woman Jesus met at the well? Because Jesus was a Jew and Jews didn't speak to Samaritans, she was shocked when He asked her for a drink of water. He said to her, "Everyone who drinks this water will be thirsty again, but whoever drinks the water I give him will never thirst. Indeed, the water I give him will become in him a spring of water welling up to eternal life" (verses 13 and 14).

Let that Living Water stir on the inside of you today, and let it spill out onto all you encounter. You never know when "a Samaritan woman" might be watching and wondering what makes you different. When she asks "for a drink," you'll be able to offer her the Living Water that you've been given. That's one beauty secret you'll want to share!

Stand by Your Man

*Don't depend on things like fancy hairdos
or gold jewelry or expensive clothes
to make you look beautiful.
Be beautiful in your heart
by being gentle and quiet.
This kind of beauty will last,
and God considers it very special.*

1 Peter 3:3–4 cev

Remember that old country song "Stand by Your Man"? (You're singing along right now, aren't you?) There's a lot of truth in that little melody. Whether you're engaged, married, or someday would like to have a special man in your life, this nugget of truth is for you. If you'll stand by your man and let him know that you are in his corner, adoring him, he will think you're the most beautiful woman in the world. Trust me!

Statistician and author Shaunti Feldhahn polled one thousand men about various topics for her book *For Women Only: What You Need to Know about the Inner Lives of Men*, so that we could better understand the men God has given us to love. When polled concerning their favorite movie scene of all time, the men overwhelmingly chose a scene from a baseball movie. You might be thinking that most men would've chosen a shoot-'em-up clip from some war movie. Not so. The most popular scene—the scene that evoked the greatest emotion from these one thousand men—came from *The Natural*. Remember that one, starring Robert Redford?

The scene goes something like this: Robert Redford is pitching, and the crowd is booing him and berating him. Redford steps off the mound and looks into the hostile crowd until his eyes lock on his woman, his gal, his love. She is quietly standing in support of him, smiling out of her eyes. In the midst of the chaos and screaming, he finds peace and strength and confidence simply by knowing she is in his corner, loving him and being proud of him.

That's what our men want. They want to know that we love them and support them—no matter what. They want to know that we still think they've got it going on. You say, "But, Michelle, I do think that. My husband knows I love him." Maybe he does, but maybe he needs to hear it more often. Or maybe he just needs to hear less criticism from you.

See, if we'll honor and adore our husbands, they'll love us like we need to be loved. It doesn't matter if our stomachs are a little pudgy or our teeth are a bit crooked; they'll see only the beauty in us. Start showing support and adoration to your man, and soon you'll become absolutely irresistible.

Bring On the Leg Warmers

Jesus Christ is the same yesterday
and today and forever.

Hebrews 13:8 NIV

Ahhh. . .the eighties. I remember them well. I graduated from Bedford, Indiana's North Lawrence High School in 1987, so I am an eighties lady. Oh yeah. I had hair so big I could hardly fit into my red Fiero. I practically had to use a can of hair spray a day to keep those big ol' bangs sky-high. I wore the neon-colored plastic bracelets up my arms—just like Madonna. And I even had a pair of leg warmers. Scary, huh? Yeah, my daughters think my senior yearbook is pretty hilarious.

Even if you're not an eighties lady, I bet there were some fashion fiascos from your time, too. For example, what was with that caked-on baby blue eye shadow of the seventies? Yuk!

Fashion trends come and go. One week, the fashion magazines say, "Long jackets are hip. The longer the better. . ." and the next week, the fashion trend reads, "Cropped, military-style jackets are the rage! Long coats are short on fashion savvy. . ." Ugh! Let's face it. It's almost impossible to keep up with the times.

Fads come and go. Styles change. And the way clothes fit our bodies definitely changes over time. (Can I hear an "Amen"?) Change is inevitable. From changing fashions to changing locations to changing diapers—as women, we're in the "changing" mode most of our lives. So in the midst of all this change, isn't it good to know that God never changes? Malachi 3:6 says, "I the Lord do not change."

You can always count on the Lord. He's there through thick and thin, leg warmers and parachute pants, and everything in between. Let Him be the stability in your life. Run to God when you feel overwhelmed by the changes going on around you. If you'll stay grounded in Him, you'll always be "heavenly hip" and ready to face anything—even if spandex stirrup pants make a comeback!

GIVE GOD CONTROL

*For I know the thoughts that I think toward you,
says the LORD, thoughts of peace and not of evil,
to give you a future and a hope.*

JEREMIAH 29:11 NKJV

We were preparing to move to Bedford, Indiana, from our Texas home, and we needed a Realtor who could really work for us. We needed a Realtor who would listen to our wants and dislikes and wholeheartedly search for the perfect home for our family. We needed Pat.

I knew we were in good hands when I called her office and her voice mail kicked on and said, "If you want to sell your home or buy a new one, don't make a move without me. . . ." I liked that! I thought, *Okay, I won't. I'm putting our home-buying experience in your hands, Pat. You are in control.* Somehow that gave me such a feeling of peace, just knowing that someone was working really hard on my behalf. Suddenly, all of the pressure was off of my shoulders. It didn't matter that I didn't know what properties were currently for sale or which homes were going to become available in the near future, because Pat was in the know. It's no wonder she has received numerous awards in the realty world. She is good at what she does, and because of her expertise, I could relax and let her do all the work. Whew! What a relief.

Well, guess what? I know someone who will

work on your behalf—His name is Jesus, and if He had voice mail, His message would say: "Don't make a move without Me...." You know what's so great about Him? He already knows your heart's desire, because He put those desires in you. And He wants to help you accomplish your dreams. He is constantly working behind the scenes for you. Isn't that a relief? See, we don't have to know everything as long as we know Him.

If you've been in the driver's seat too long, move over and let Jesus get behind the wheel. Let Him take total control of your life. If you do, you'll experience peace and satisfaction. You'll feel true joy just knowing that the Lord is on your side, desiring the very best for you. He'll lead you into good decisions. He'll guide you away from troubled times. He may even help you find your dream home! Your job? Let go and let God. In other words, don't make a move without the Lord. He has a *beautiful* life planned for you!

WHO'S TOO OLD?

*"I kept thinking, 'Experience will tell.
The longer you live, the wiser you become.'"*

JOB 32:7 MSG

Bible teacher Darlene Bishop said in one of her latest taped teachings, "God called me to teach the Word when I was only fourteen years old. I knew it. I heard that still small voice. But I didn't preach my first sermon until I was thirty-eight years old." She went on to say that she's now in her early sixties, and she's more effective for God than she's ever been before. She's teaching more places, writing more books, and touching more lives than she ever thought possible. Bottom line—you're not too old to do what God has called you to do.

Today's society would have you believe that women past thirty should be put out to pasture. But that's simply not the case. God isn't concerned about our age, our wrinkles, or any gray hairs that might be sprouting. He just needs a willing vessel with a faithful heart.

Take Sarah in the Bible, for example. Abraham's wife thought she was too old to bear Abraham an heir. By the world's standards, she was well past childbearing years. Physically, it was impossible for her to conceive a child. But God had given her and Abraham a promise—that Abraham would be the father of many nations. God didn't need Sarah's youthful body to produce a child. God just needed her faith and her willingness to be used. Once those were in place, she birthed Isaac—the promised heir.

Maybe you look into the mirror and see a woman who is too old to do anything worthwhile. Maybe you've bought the lie that the devil has been whispering in your ear: "You're too old to accomplish anything for God. Life has already passed you by. No one cares what an old woman has to say." If that's you, stop listening to the devil. He's a liar. You are not too old to do what God has planned for you. Like Darlene, you may be entering into your greatest days. We may be too old by Hollywood's standards, but we're just right by God's standards.

If you want to feel better about your mature appearance, you can color over your gray hair. You can even use antiwrinkle cream to combat those lines on your face. But you don't have to do those things to please God. He doesn't need a line-free face to do His work—only a willing heart. You're the perfect age to do what God has called you to do. So go for it!

No More Bug Juice

But when the Holy Spirit controls our lives,
he will produce this kind of fruit in us:
love, joy, peace, patience, kindness, goodness,
faithfulness, gentleness, and self-control.
GALATIANS 5:22–23 NLT

All of the gals in our Bible study have a secret saying we use to keep each other in line. When one of us starts acting ugly, a loving sister in Christ will whisper, "Bug juice." The meaning behind it? Well, when you squash a bug, what comes out? Bug juice! And believe me, it ain't pretty!

In other words, when we're under pressure, whatever is on the inside of us is what will come out. If it's bug juice, that's what spews out. If it's love, joy, peace, patience, kindness, goodness, faithfulness, gentleness, and self-control—that's what comes out. That's why we need to spend much time in the Word of God, filling ourselves with more of Jesus and His promises.

Not long ago, my friend Susan was able to put this "bug juice" principle to the test when her daughter, Schalen, was in a very serious automobile accident. When Schalen was admitted into intensive care with a broken neck and blood clots on the brain—panic filled the waiting room. The situation looked very bleak. As the doctors shared the severity of Schalen's injuries with the family, Susan stood strong. Through tears, she declared, "I will not fear. God is in control. Schalen is healed in Jesus' name!"

When the pressure of the situation pressed heavy upon Susan, no bug juice oozed out. The only thing coming out of Susan was faith-filled words. She quoted scriptures and praised God for Schalen's whole and strong body.

Susan's positive attitude and faith-filled statements changed the entire atmosphere of that waiting room. In less than twenty-four hours, Schalen rounded the corner. In forty-eight hours, they had her up and walking. Only a week later, Schalen walked across the stage at Bedford North Lawrence High School to accept her diploma.

Maybe you are in a high-pressure situation right now, and bug juice is about to blow! Ask God to develop the fruit of the Spirit on the inside of you. Spend some time today in God's Word. Meditate on His promises, and rest in Him. Pretty soon, bug juice will be a thing of the past and only beautiful love and faith will flow out of you. You'll emanate Jesus' love when the pressure is on. And like Susan, you'll change the atmosphere around you. There's already enough bug juice out there. Why not fill your world with beauty today?

BE CONSISTENT, GET RESULTS

"Study this Book of the Law continually.
Meditate on it day and night so you
may be sure to obey all that is written in it. Only
then will you succeed."
JOSHUA 1:8 NLT

Gorgeous singer and actress Beyonce was recently asked to share one of her top beauty secrets in a woman's beauty magazine. In the article, she said, "Never go to bed with your makeup on. I always make sure I wash my face before turning in for the night."

Beyonce, of course, is known for her gorgeous skin. Oprah Winfrey once commented that Beyonce's skin was like butter. Hollywood makeup artists have shared that they've never seen such naturally gorgeous skin on any actress. Because her skin is so great, they rarely have to cover any blemishes. So when Beyonce shared a beauty secret about maintaining great skin, I was interested to hear what she had to say.

Her advice seemed so simple—wash your face every night. Sure, that seems easy. But when you're supertired and you just want to drop into bed and call it a day, the walk to the bathroom sink can seem like a million-mile journey. And if your skin-care routine has a few steps—such as washing, exfoliating, masking, toning, and moisturizing—it's a time commitment, as well.

But what happens if you don't wash your face each night? Well, the makeup soaks into your pores and remains there overnight. Instead of giving your face the opportunity to breathe and heal overnight, you basically contaminate it while you sleep. After a few nights of neglect, your face will not look so good. You'll probably have more fine lines, several blemishes, and a rough texture to your skin. Bottom line—you can't neglect your skin and expect glowing results.

It's the same way with inner beauty. You can't neglect your time in the Word or your prayer time and expect glowing results. It just doesn't work that way. After a few days of neglect, your inner beauty will begin to show some cracks, some blemishes, and some roughness. We need to wash ourselves in God's Word every day. Then people will want to know *our* inner beauty secrets, and we can say, "First, let Jesus cleanse your heart from all sin. Second, wash yourself in His Word every single day. Third, spend time in prayer and allow His love to flow into you and out of you."

So go ahead. Wash, exfoliate, mask, tone, and moisturize your face on a regular basis. But don't neglect your inner beauty. Make the commitment to become more beautiful inside and out!

LEARNING TO LISTEN

"Be still, and know that I am God."

PSALM 46:10 NIV

Let's face it. We like to talk. The *Farmer's Almanac* reports that the average woman speaks twenty-five thousand more words per day than the average man. No wonder the men in our lives "tune us out" from time to time.

Listening is almost a lost art form today. The late Brenda Ueland, a prolific Minnesota author and columnist, once wrote: "We should all know this: that listening, not talking, is the gifted and great role, and the imaginative role. And the true listener is much more beloved and magnetic than the talker, and she is more effective and learns more and does more good."

My friend Darlene recently learned how attractive good listening skills can be. She sat next to a woman at her son's ball game, and since she'd never met the woman before, Darlene asked her several questions. The woman answered her inquiries all night long—never once asking Darlene to share any information in return. Later that week, the gabby woman's daughter told Darlene how much her mother had enjoyed their conversation at the ball game. Darlene had to smile at the daughter's comment. It had been a one-sided conversation, but apparently it was just what the woman had needed, and Darlene was glad to have obliged.

Many times, we're so eager to share our witty comments or tell a funny story to make ourselves seem more attractive that we don't actually listen to the speaker. No, we're too busy "rehearsing" our responses in our minds, waiting for the first opportunity to interrupt and dazzle those around us.

Are you guilty of interrupting? Do you lack listening skills? If you're like most women, you do. And that's not a very attractive trait. No matter how pretty you might be on the outside, if you're constantly interrupting and talking over others, people will not see you in a good light. People love a good listener—especially the men in our lives. If you'll hang on his every word, he'll talk to you more often.

Practice listening today. You just might learn that talking is way overrated.

SET THE RIGHT TONE

Your godly lives will speak to them
better than any words. They will be won
over by watching your pure, godly behavior.
1 PETER 3:1–2 NLT

Remember when you first started dating your significant other? You couldn't wait to see each other. You thought he was so handsome, and he thought you were absolutely gorgeous. It was butterflies and sunshine every time you were together, right? Then...something happened. Suddenly, the little quirky habits you thought were so cute about one another weren't so cute anymore. He began acting distant, and you began nagging. After a while he didn't seem quite so handsome, and now he rarely tells you that you're beautiful.

That's where many couples find themselves today, which is why many women feel so unattractive and depressed. Women's magazines tell us to spice up our relationship with new negligees. So we run to Victoria's Secret and realize that only Victoria looks good in most of those outfits. Just how do we become attractive again to that person who used to adore us?

We have to set the right tone.

When Jeff and I married, we quickly discovered that we didn't love everything about each other—at least not all of the time. It was one of those days when I settled into my chair at women's Bible study. I sulked as Monda, our teacher, began her lesson on 1 Peter 3.

Oh, no, I thought. *Not the "submission lesson." Not today!*

Monda began by saying, "Wives, *you* set the tone in the home." I never heard much past that statement because that one nugget of truth grabbed hold of my heart and wouldn't let go. I realized that I didn't have to look like Angelina Jolie to be attractive to my mate. It wasn't even about my appearance. It was about my attitude toward my mate. I decided that day to take Monda's words of wisdom and apply them to my home. Instead of nagging, I would find reasons to compliment my mate. Instead of just saying good-bye in the morning, I would give him a big kiss to start the day. Guess what? Things got better immediately.

No, I don't get it right every day, but after fourteen years of marriage, I'm a much better tone setter than I used to be! If your spouse is less than crazy about you as of late, or if you long to have your husband look at you the way he once did—through adoring eyes—you have to change your attitude. Meditate on 1 Peter 3 and begin setting the right tone today. Soon your home will be heavenly and your husband will refer to you as "his beautiful angel."

BLIND FAITH

*I am sure that nothing can separate us from
God's love—not life or death, not angels
or spirits, not the present or the future.*

ROMANS 8:38 CEV

L et's be honest. There are some beauty tricks that simply don't make sense if you think about them too long. In fact, some of them are downright gross. For instance, if you have tired, puffy eyes from too many sleepless nights, you're supposed to pat a little Preparation H under your eyes to reduce the puffiness and rejuvenate your tired peepers. Yes, it's quite effective, but did you ever think you'd use hemorrhoid cream around your eyes? Me, either! Or how about the old Vaseline-on-the-teeth trick? Beauty queens have known about this tip for years! You simply put a little slimy Vaseline over your front teeth to create a shinier smile onstage. Of course, it feels yucky, but it works!

Sometimes you just have to have blind faith and try these odd beauty tricks. There's no rhyme or reason to them, and they may even seem gross to you. But if you try them, you'll discover they actually work.

You know, some of the teachings in the Bible seem odd, too. Take Matthew 5:38–44 (niv), for example. Instead of an "eye for eye, and tooth for tooth," we are supposed to love our enemies: "You have heard that it was said, 'Eye for eye, and tooth for tooth.' But I tell you, Do not resist an evil person. If someone strikes you on the right cheek, turn to him the other also. And if someone wants to sue you and take your tunic, let him have your cloak as well. If someone forces you to go one mile, go with him two miles. . . . Love your enemies and pray for those who persecute you."

Hmm. Not exactly what human nature tells us to do, right? Sometimes you just have to trust and go forward in blind faith. If you're a very practical person, this might be hard for you, so ask God to help you follow His ways even when they seem outlandish or uncomfortable. He will! He is the Father of faith, and He has more than enough to fill you up so that you can step out in blind faith and love your enemies, pray for those who despitefully use you, and go that extra mile.

So take a risk. Go against your human nature and step out in blind faith both in the natural and the spiritual. You'll have rested eyes, shiny teeth, and a beautiful spirit!

GOD LOVES YOU—
FLAWS AND ALL

*So let's come near God with pure hearts and
a confidence that comes from having faith.*
HEBREWS 10:22 CEV

If you listen closely, you can hear them. Women around the globe, groaning and moaning in dressing rooms. Are they in pain? Are they ill? No, it's just bathing suit season, and they're trying to find the one perfect suit that doesn't make them look fat. It's a quest every woman embarks on, and it's one of the most daunting tasks she will ever face.

Seriously, is there anything more humbling than standing in front of a dressing room mirror, under those unforgiving fluorescent lights, trying on bathing suit after bathing suit? I think not. I dread it every year. Because no matter how many miles you've logged in previous months, no matter how many crunches you've crunched, no matter how many desserts you've passed up, bathing suits show every imperfection. While you might be able to hide a few dimples underneath blue jeans or a nice black dress, you're not hiding anything in a bathing suit.

That's pretty much how it is with God. You might be able to fake grin your way through church. You might be able to "play Christian" in front of your friends and family. But when you enter the throne room, it's like wearing your bathing suit before God. You can't hide any imperfections from Him. He sees it all. That truth used to horrify me—even more than trying on bathing suits—but not anymore.

Here's the great thing about God. He gave us Jesus to take care of our sin, because God knew we'd be flawed. No matter how many good deeds we do, no matter how many chapters of the Bible we read each day, and no matter how many casseroles we bake for church functions, we can never be good enough for God. We can't earn our way into God's favor. All we have to do is ask Jesus to be the Lord of our lives, and we're "in." Then, whenever we enter the throne room, God sees us through "the Jesus filter," and all He sees is perfection. If you haven't asked Jesus to take away your sin and be the Lord of your life, why not take care of that today? It's the most wonderful step you'll ever make.

Now, if we could just figure out some kind of perfection filter for bathing suit season, life would be super.

A Winning Look

*No, in all these things we are more than
conquerors through him who loved us.*

ROMANS 8:37 NIV

Ahh. . .the dreaded last word. Are you a gotta-have-the-last-word kind of gal? Do you always have to be right? If so, you're not alone. I am also a member of that club, and let me tell you, it's a pretty lonely and sad membership. When you always have to be right, people tend to shy away from you. They will conveniently have an excuse "not to see you" every time you want to get together. And can we blame them? What our mothers used to tell us is really true—pretty is as pretty does. If you act ugly, people will view you as ugly, and they won't want to be around you.

So if we know that having to have the last word makes us unattractive, why do we continue in this behavior? Because we are taught that winning is everything. We're taught, "Nice guys (and gals) finish last." We're told, "If you don't look out for number one, who will?" But those teachings are directly opposed to the Word of God.

Don't get me wrong—Jesus is all about winning, but not at someone else's expense. The Bible says that He has made us more than conquerors. (Sounds like God is in the business of making winners, doesn't it?) He wants us to succeed, but He wants us to do it His way. When we do it His way, we'll still have friends when we arrive at that all-important winner's circle.

So stop looking out for "number one" and start looking to *the* One! Let Him mold you into the beautiful creature He's created you to be! Determine to change your ugly ways. Realize that you don't have to get the last word in. His Word is word enough. And begin following in Jesus' footsteps. His steps always lead to victory, and you'll look good on the journey!

BRING ON THE BREAKTHROUGHS!

And I am sure that God,
who began the good work within you,
will continue his work until it is finally finished
on that day when Christ Jesus comes back again.
PHILIPPIANS 1:6 NLT

My mother-in-law has used Merle Norman cosmetics for many years. Trends in cosmetics come and go, but Martha sticks with her tried-and-true line. Sure, over the years she's tried products from other beauty companies, but she always returns to her favorite—Merle Norman.

Women are funny about those kinds of things. When we get used to something and it works for us, we are very resistant to change. Even if a beauty breakthrough occurs, even if a "new and improved" line is launched, and even if our best friend starts selling a different product line, we'd rather just stick with what we've been using for years. Like the old expression goes: "If it ain't broke, why fix it?"

While this line of thinking might be okay when it comes to our cosmetic choices, it can be quite dangerous in the spiritual realm. A few years ago I was attending a traditional denominational church and a battle in the vestibule broke out. We'd hired a new music minister, and he was full of energy and new ideas. Instead of only leading the congregation in hymns from our tattered old red hymnbooks, he began leading us in contemporary worship choruses. All of us thirty and younger loved the new contemporary worship, while most of the elder members—not so much. It became a clash of the choruses. The elderly population was adamantly against the worship music shift. One of the board members finally spoke up and said, "We've sung these hymns for years. If they were good enough for the founders of this church, they're good enough for me."

Eventually, the bright-eyed praise and worship leader was forced to lead the congregation in old hymns—period. It caused great division in our congregation, and several families left the church due to the immense tension.

As Christians we need to be open to new things—as long as those new things are of God. Ask God to give you discernment so that you can go with the flow as long as that flow is from the Father. Don't be resistant to change. Maybe God is trying to help you grow in an area but your resistance is slowing up the process. I say, bring on the beauty breakthroughs and latest skin-care technology, and bring on the new spiritual revelations and levels of maturity. We're on our way to becoming better—inside and out!

A Beautiful New You

Anyone who belongs to Christ is a new person.
The past is forgotten, and everything is new.

2 Corinthians 5:17 CEV

I recently saw an infomercial for a skin-care system called ProActiv that is guaranteed to help those who suffer from acne. During this infomercial, a skin-care specialist explained how blemishes start beneath the skin two weeks before they ever manifest on one's face. That's why, she said, we should treat acne before it shows itself on the surface. By treating the pimples before they ever show up on the surface of the skin, the skin is consistently clear. Problem skin becomes a thing of the past. Testimonial after testimonial confirmed that the products worked. Finally, I was convinced. I ordered the products for my "tweenage" daughters, hoping to help them avoid the perils of pimples that typically go along with adolescence.

You know, products like ProActiv may take care of the pimples that pop up on our faces and bodies, but the Word of God takes care of the blemishes of the heart. And you don't have to order it off of an infomercial. It's free, and it's for you! Hurt and bitterness are much like those hidden pimples that lie deep beneath the surface. They may lie dormant for weeks, but eventually they will pop out and cause all kinds of problems.

If you've been harboring hurt or buried bitterness in your heart, let God's Word go to the root of those issues and zap them. If you don't, hurt feelings will present themselves at the most inopportune times. Hurt will rear its ugly head— just when you think you've gotten rid of it forever. So read God's Word on a regular basis and keep your heart continually clear. If you don't, hurt and bitterness and all of its ugly buddies will erupt in your life again and again and again. Don't let that happen! Be proactive! Get in the Word of God and unveil a more beautiful version of you!

STEP INTO YOUR DREAMS

*This resurrection life you received from
God is not a timid, grave-tending life.
It's adventurously expectant, greeting God
with a childlike "What's next, Papa?"*
ROMANS 8:15 MSG

In the early 1950s, Lillian Vernon spent five hundred dollars on her first advertisement, offering monogrammed belts and handbags. That one little ad, that one little risk, produced a $32,000 profit! Today—more than fifty years later—Lillian Vernon is still selling gift items and personalized goodies through a very successful catalog sales program. In fact, her company now generates more than $250 million in sales every year. Now that's a lot of handbags! She has quite a success story.

But what if Lillian Vernon hadn't run that small ad? Back then, five hundred dollars was a lot of money to spend with no guarantee of recouping it. What if she hadn't taken that risk? Well, she wouldn't be a millionaire, and lots of folks would have to find another catalog to use for their annual Christmas shopping.

Maybe God has put a dream in your heart that is so big you haven't even shared it with anyone. Maybe God is directing you to take a risk in business or start your own Bible study or volunteer for your child's school or run for office. So what's stopping you? Why aren't you running that ad like Lillian Vernon? Why aren't you going for it?

If you're like most women, fear is holding you back. Fear is a very real emotion. It can get a grip on you that won't let go—until you make it let go through the Word of God. The Bible tells us that "God has not given us a spirit of fear." So if it didn't come from God, where did it come from? Satan, maybe? You bet. So get rid of that nasty old emotion. Say out loud, "I can do all things through Christ who strengthens me. I am the head and not the tail. I am more than a conqueror."

Remind yourself of who you are in Christ Jesus on a daily basis. You are a child of the Most High King. You have the mind of Christ. God has crowned you with His favor. And those are just a few of the promises in His Word. So grab hold of God's promises, put fear behind you, and step into your dreams. Pretty soon, you'll be sharing your success story!

"Don't Hate Me because I'm Beautiful"

Yet you are stupid enough to brag,
and it is wrong to be so proud.

James 4:16 CEV

You've seen the commercial. The gorgeous girl whips her long, luscious locks to the side, then with her pouty, very glossy lips, she utters, "Don't hate me because I'm beautiful."

But in reality, we would hate her—not because she's beautiful. No, we'd hate her because she loves to brag on herself. Let's face it; nobody likes a bragger. (You're thinking of someone right now, aren't you?) We all know someone like that girl in the commercial. She might not be as blatant, but you can bet your lipstick she'll find a way to sneak in a boast or two.

She might not even brag about herself. She might brag about her new home. Or worse, she might drone on and on about her super-accomplished kids. (Her car bumpers are covered with My Kid Is an Honor Student stickers. Okay, I have those bumper stickers, too. Sorry.) No matter what she brags about, it's enough to make you want to run for the hills. Am I right?

Let me ask you another question. Are you a bragger? Do you love talking on and on about yourself? It's an easy habit to fall into, but it's also a very dangerous one. The Bible says that pride comes before a fall, and that fall may plop you right into a pit of loneliness. Friends will start avoiding you. Family members will dread your annual brag letter, er um, Christmas letter. People will hate you—but it won't be because you're beautiful. So don't go there!

If you're struggling with the bad habit of bragging, ask God to put a watch over your mouth. Make a conscious decision to listen more than you talk. And more than anything, learn to trust God to raise you up. You'll discover that you won't have to brag on yourself to feel important. God has a big ol' brag book, and He will find ways to lift you up and give you favor with those around you. You'll win friends and influence people, and they'll love you because you're beautiful on the inside. After all, that's where it really counts!

Singing the
Blue Jeans Blues

Not that I have already obtained all this,
or have already been made perfect,
but I press on to take hold of that
for which Christ Jesus took hold of me.
Philippians 3:12 NIV

We've all been there. You go to the mall with high hopes and high self-esteem, ready to buy a new pair of jeans. Seventy-two pairs later, your legs are raw from trying them on and your self-esteem is lower than a snake's belly. Sadly, you leave the mall, determined to work out seven times a day and eat only lettuce until the next time you get the courage to try on jeans once again.

Jeans are a part of every gal's wardrobe, but finding a pair that fits every curve and hides every bulge can be quite challenging. Wouldn't it be great if jeans were labeled something like this: "If you have short legs, these jeans are for you," or "If your thighs are heavy, try these." Okay, so the marketing pitch might need a little work, but honest labels would enable women of every build to find the right jeans.

Still, we press on—determined to find the jeans that won't make our hind ends look flat and wide. Sometimes this quest may take days, even weeks. But, eventually, we will succeed. We're women—shopping challenges don't faze us.

If only we were that determined and stead-fast when it comes to other areas of our lives—especially spiritual battles. If you're like me, you sometimes get weary in the well-doing. Have you found yourself throwing in the faith towel before you see your victory come to pass?

It's easy to do. Evangelist Chip Brim once shared that God had shown him a vision of Christians on a football field. They were all collapsing on the one-yard line. They were so close to their breakthroughs, but they simply grew weary and quit just inches from their victory.

Chip said it made him very sad to see so many Christians giving up on their dreams or quitting before they'd realized their breakthroughs. I've got news for you. It makes God sad, too. He longs to see His children walk in abundance in every area of their lives. He has already paid the price for your victory! You just have to push toward that goal—no matter how hard it gets. The Bible says all things are possible for those who love the Lord. The Bible says you can do all things through Christ Jesus. Don't quit just short of your victory. The end zone is in sight! And the reward is even better than finding that perfect pair of blue jeans. So don't give up!

A SELFLESS VESSEL

Love cares more for others than for self.
1 CORINTHIANS 13:4 MSG

My neighbor Melanie is definitely a dog lover. She and her husband have two "little boys"—Rupert and Jackson. They are the most adorable little fluff balls you've ever seen. And let me tell you, these puppies are treated like royalty. I often meet the couple taking "the boys" on their evening jaunt, and we'll chat about our precious puppies. (I have three adorable miniature long-haired dachshunds.)

Not long ago, Melanie told me that she had decided to adopt a little girl dog to join in the fun. She had seen a Humane Society advertisement in the local paper, and this little poodle mix named Peaches had captured Mel's heart. She went on to say, "I couldn't bear the thought of this little poodle being put down." So Mel adopted Peaches and took her to the veterinarian for all of her necessary shots. As it turned out, Peaches had a bad case of kennel cough, so Mel had to leave her at the vet's for a week or so. But every single day, Mel would go to the vet's office and play with Peaches, petting her and talking nice to her. She wanted Peaches to know she would be loved at her new home. The two bonded.

On the day that Mel was supposed to bring

Peaches home, she overheard the veterinarian talking to a woman who was looking for a dog to be a companion for her elderly father. He lived in a retirement home, and his beloved cocker spaniel had recently passed away, leaving him very lonely and depressed. As Mel listened to the woman's story, she knew what she had to do. Peaches was needed somewhere else—even though Mel already loved that little poodle as if she'd owned her for years.

As the delighted and grateful woman left the veterinarian's office with Peaches under her arm, Mel sobbed. But she wasn't crying because she was sad. She was crying tears of joy because she knew God had truly used her that day. She had been the selfless vessel He needed to make an old man's dream come true.

A selfless heart is a rare and beautiful thing today, but you can always spot the ones who have such hearts. They seem to glow with goodness. So have you done any selfless acts lately? Are you available to be that selfless vessel for God? In this dog-eat-dog world, God needs us to glow with goodness. Be a selfless vessel today.

BLOSSOM WHERE YOU'RE PLANTED

There is a time for everything,
a season for every activity under heaven.
ECCLESIASTES 3:1 NLT

I have a friend named Barbie who is an excellent writer. She currently works as a columnist/reporter for a daily newspaper. It's a high-stress job. The newsroom is a frantic, wonderful, wacky place to work. I know because I used to work at that same daily newspaper several years ago. Deadlines loom. Bosses demand. And the news never stops. The news doesn't care if your daughter has a dance recital. It still has to be written right away. Being a newspaper reporter is the worst job you'll ever love. Long hours. Disgruntled readers. Difficult sources. You'll deal with them all on a daily basis, but at the end of the day, you'll know you've contributed to a greater cause. You'll know you've made a difference. If just one person is touched by a story you wrote for page B-3, then it was all worth it.

Still, it's tough. There are days when my friend longs to escape the daily rat race and write Christian books and children's stories from her home office. But there is a season for everything, and Barbie is blooming right where she is planted. She isn't blatant about her faith, but you can just tell when you read her stories that there's a Christian pecking away at that computer. Her stories touch your heart, make you think, and challenge you to be a better person.

Let me ask you—are you blooming where you're planted? If your dream is to stay home with your children and yet you're stuck in a customer service job somewhere, are you blossoming on the job? Do you smile and earnestly try to help your customers, or do you grumble around, complaining that you'd rather be home with your babies? No matter what season of life you're in, you should bloom. Ask God to help you do the best you can. Ask Him to help you be a blessing wherever you are. Ask God to give you the patience and love to blossom—even if you're among a bunch of ungodly weeds. Just think, you might be the only Christian those weeds will ever see.

Joyce Meyer once said, "Enjoy the journey on the way to where you're going." That's good advice. You'll be a lot happier, and you'll be a lot more attractive to those who are around you. So go ahead—bloom!

No Divas Allowed!

"Here is a simple,
rule-of-thumb guide for behavior:
Ask yourself what you want people to do for you,
then grab the initiative and do it for them."
MATTHEW 7:12 MSG

Do you love to read gossip magazines? You know, the ones on the racks right by the checkout lanes in the grocery store? I confess—I read them. And do you know what is in most every issue? A diva report. These tabloid journalists follow stars around and let us know which stars are nice and which ones are dastardly divas. You discover which stars care very little about "the little people" and which famous folks do very nice things for the people in their lives—even those who serve them.

I am a huge Doris Day fan. When I was pregnant with my daughter Abby, I was sentenced to bed rest for several weeks due to premature labor. One can just watch so many TV talk shows, and the medicine I had to take in order to stop the contractions made it almost impossible to focus on words in a book. So reading was out. Then my mother brought over as many Doris Day movies as she could find, and I watched them over and over again. From *Move Over Darling* with James Garner to *That Touch of Mink* starring Cary Grant—my days were filled with Doris Day and her wonderful movies until I finally welcomed Abby Leigh into this world. Afterward, I wrote a thank-you note to Doris. I just wanted to tell her how much her movies had meant to me during those long days of bed rest. I certainly never expected a response, but I got one. Doris Day sent me a lovely handwritten note telling me how much my note had touched her. Wow!

Certainly Doris Day didn't have to take time to thank me, but she did. I cherish that note. No, I'm not an obsessed fan. I keep the note because it reminds me to take time for other people. This world would be a much better place if we all operated by the Golden Rule: "Do unto others as you would have them do unto you."

Are you a diva? Or do you take time for other people? Remember the Golden Rule the next time you're in line at a fast-food restaurant and the little gal behind the counter gives you the wrong order. If you're more like a diva than a Doris Day, ask the Lord to help you become more like Him.

BRONZED BEAUTY

*Those who live according to the sinful nature
have their minds set on what that nature desires;
but those who live in accordance with the Spirit
have their minds set on what the Spirit desires.*

ROMANS 8:5 NIV

There's one thing about Texans: We love to be tan. Sun worshipers can be found throughout the world, but there are a great many of these bronzed beauties in the Lone Star State. It seems there is a tanning salon on almost every corner. I'll admit, I love to be tan, too. I'd much rather show off healthy, tan-looking legs instead of milky white ones. How about you? Funny thing about tanning. . . While it makes you look healthy, tanned skin is actually a sign of sun damage.

When your skin absorbs the sun's rays, those rays actually damage the DNA in your skin's cells. This damage causes the cells to become dysfunctional, according to Michele Grodberg, MD, who is quoted in an article titled "Can You Reverse Sun Damage?" on msn.com online. And those dysfunctional cells behave improperly, resulting in a reduction in the production of collagen and elastin, a thinning of the top layer of skin, a halt in the skin's natural ability to slough off its dead layers, and a rise in pigmentation. Ultimately, these dysfunctional cells can become cancerous.

Even though we now know that sunbathing isn't good for us—and even though we know that skin cancer is the most prevalent cancer of all cancers—still, some women are willing to risk their health and even their lives to have that healthy-looking bronzed body. We will risk it all for a quick tanning fix. We want to look good now, even if it means we'll have to live with sun-damaged skin later.

Sin is the same way. The devil will make it seem very attractive to you right now, but ultimately, it leads to death. Sin will always take you further than you wanted to go, keep you longer than you wanted to stay, and cost you more than you were willing to pay. So don't go there! Don't compromise your faith for a quick sin fix. They call women who sunbathe "sun worshipers." But that's the wrong kind of sun worshiper. We need to be SON worshipers. We may not be bronzed, but we'll definitely be beautiful in Him!

DON'T SETTLE

I will bless you with a future filled with hope—a future of success, not of suffering.

JEREMIAH 29:11 CEV

In the movie *Monster-in-law* starring Jane Fonda and Jennifer Lopez, JLo plays a single gal named Charlie. She's never had much luck in love, so she's skeptical of most men. Then she meets Dr. Wonderful at a party. She thinks he must be too good to be true, so she moves forward very cautiously.

When he brings her coffee at the beach one morning, she asks him, "Why should I go out with you?" He answers, "Because I'm different." Before he can say anything, she turns her back to him and asks, "Okay, then, what color are my eyes?" He doesn't even hesitate and answers, "They're brown at first glance. But upon further inspection, they have amber flecks in them...and when you look into the sunlight, they appear almost green. That's my favorite."

She turns to face him, smiling, and says, "I would have settled for *brown*."

It was a cute bit of dialogue, but in reality, women are often prone to settling for less than the best. Somehow, we've been deceived into thinking we don't deserve the very best. This is especially true if you've ever been verbally or physically abused.

Bible teacher Joyce Meyer has often shared

how she always felt that she didn't deserve happiness due to the abuse in her background. Eventually, she realized that was a lie of the devil and began seeking God's best in every area of her life. Today, she is on the front lines for Jesus, bringing millions of people into the kingdom of God. But just think if she would have settled for less than God had for her.

So what are you settling for in your life? Have you given up on God's best? Or is there something in your past that makes you think you don't deserve happiness, love, wholeness, and a beautiful life? Listen, if you've accepted Jesus as your Lord and Savior, your slate is totally wiped clean. No matter what you've done or what someone else has done to you—you are valuable to God and He desires good things for you. He wants to give you beauty for ashes—what a deal!

If you've been settling for much less than what God has promised you in His Word, it's not too late. Start expecting God's beauty in your life. Ask Him to help you realize just how precious you are to Him. Once you know that truth, you'll never settle again!

Happiness Is
a Beautiful Thing

A happy heart makes the face cheerful. . . .
The cheerful heart has a continual feast.
Proverbs 15:13, 15 niv

My mother has always been a happy person. It didn't matter if it was raining outside. It didn't matter if our air-conditioning went out in mid-July. It didn't matter if one of her friends talked ugly to her. Mom has always chosen happiness.

Growing up, Mom's happiness bugged me. She'd begin each day something like this. She'd burst into my bedroom, flip on my light switch, and begin her very loud rendition of "This is the day that the Lord has made. Let us rejoice and be glad in it." She'd sing at the top of her lungs and occasionally clap in time, as well. What a way to start the day, eh? There was no sleeping in at our house, because if you didn't get up, she'd just start another verse!

After my father passed away last year, I didn't hear my mom singing anymore. I worried about her. I prayed to God, "Please restore the song back into my mother's life." After a period of grieving, little by little, I saw Mom's happiness return. It started with a hum, and now she's all-out singing again. I'm still waiting for that loud clapping to return, but I'm sure it's in the works. Why? Because Mom doesn't base her happiness on her circumstances. Sure, she's lonely without

Daddy, but she chooses to be happy because of Jesus. She chooses to focus on the beauty in life—not the tragedy.

How is your happiness level? If it has been awhile since you've burst forth in song, give it a whirl! Sing praises unto God until you sing yourself happy. But you say, "Michelle, you don't know what I'm going through right now. There's no way I can be happy." You may be right. But through Jesus you *can* be happy. Job 8:21 in the New King James Version of the Bible says, "He will yet fill your mouth with laughing, and your lips with rejoicing." That's a promise you can count on! He will—but you have to want it. You have to choose happiness.

Comic writer Robert Orben once said, "Happiness is contagious. Be a carrier!" That's pretty good advice. If you choose to be happy, you'll discover more people will want to be around you. Being happy simply makes you more attractive. Your happiness will be infectious. Happiness will become a lifelong habit, as it has been for my mom. You may even find yourself humming happily all day long. Beware: Loud clapping is soon to follow! Go ahead—choose happiness today! It's a beautiful life!

STEP INTO THE LIGHT

"This is the crisis we're in:
God-light streamed into the world, but men
and women everywhere ran for the darkness.
They went for the darkness because they were
not really interested in pleasing God."

JOHN 3:19 MSG

Have you ever been in a situation where you've had to do your makeup in a dim room? Sometimes when I travel, the lighting in the hotel room isn't so great. I put on my makeup as best I can, but when I get into the car and look at myself in the bright sunlight, I am horrified. Many times, I have on way too much blush or eye makeup, but because of the dark hotel room, I had no idea I looked like Bozo in drag. I thought I was looking pretty good, but the natural light told me differently. Light is a powerful thing. It reveals much about us. This is also true in spiritual matters.

The Bible says that Jesus is the Light of the World. When we look to Him and His Word, it also reveals much about us. Through His Word you may find areas of darkness in your life that you weren't even aware existed. The Lord may shine His light on bitterness that's been hiding in a dark corner of your heart. Or the Lord may shine His light on that unforgiveness you've been harboring for years. If you've been living in darkness for some time, looking into the Light of the Word of God can be quite scary! You'll see many flaws in yourself. (You may find that you also look like Bozo in drag, spiritually speaking.)

But don't run from Jesus and the Bible when you see your flaws and shortcomings. Instead, embrace the truth and ask Him to get rid of the flaws that He exposed. God wants you to live free from that mess. That's why He has illuminated the situation for you. Finding out you have areas that need work is the first step to recovery, right?

Let Jesus and His light fill you up and flow out of you. Continue to look into the Word and allow His light to reveal areas where you need growth. As you do this, you'll find that you are being transformed from Bozo to Beauty. Talk about an extreme makeover! Bring it on!

CLEAN OUT YOUR CLOSET

What this means is that those who
become Christians become new persons.
They are not the same anymore,
for the old life is gone.
A new life has begun!
2 CORINTHIANS 5:17 NLT

O kay, I admit it. My closet is a mess. I have way too many clothes and not enough closet space. And to be honest, there are many outfits in there that I'll never wear again. Many women find themselves in this dilemma. But not my friend Ally. Whenever she buys something new, she simply gives away something else in her closet. (I am quite thrilled with her system, because I have been the recipient of many of her castoffs. From Chanel handbags to Nike workout wear, Ally gives great stuff away.) That keeps her closet from becoming too crowded.

I have yet another friend named Dana who should be renamed "closet organizer extraordinaire." She organizes closets by season, color, and occasion. It's amazing, really. Her rule is this: If you haven't worn something in the past year, it goes. Like Ally, Dana gets rid of something old and makes room for something new. This keeps her color-coded closet from getting cluttered.

That principle works the same way in our spiritual lives. God is a God of order. Before we can put on new things, we have to do away with the old, outdated, and sinful things. If our spiritual lives are cluttered with things like lying, unforgiveness, unwholesome talk, bitterness, anger, or anything else that doesn't match God's attributes, we have to get rid of them to make room for more of God.

Your closet may not be cluttered with bad stuff. In fact, it might be totally jam-packed with good things, but if those things aren't what God has for you right now, they are clutter. They are as outdated as those parachute pants in the back of your closet. For instance, maybe heading up the vacation Bible school program at your church for the past five years was a very good thing. But if it was just for a season, and now God wants you to hand that duty off to someone else because He has a new thing for you to do, it's clutter!

How long has it been since you've cleaned out your spiritual closet? Have you been hanging on to things for far too long? If so, get rid of those things. Ask God to help you clean out your closet. He is the Master at organization, and He can't wait to see you wearing all of the new stuff He has for you!

WHAT'S HOLDING YOU BACK?

Thank you for making me
so wonderfully complex!
Your workmanship is marvelous—
and how well I know it.

PSALM 139:14 NLT

Fanny Crosby, the author of more than nine thousand hymns and another one thousand secular poems and songs, never let her physical challenges stop the call she felt on her life. And she never let her disability become a hindrance in her relationship with God.

Born in 1820, Fanny had her vision at birth. But at six weeks, she suffered an eye inflammation. The family's usual doctor wasn't available, so they sought help from a man who claimed to be medically qualified to help. He put a poultice on Fanny's eyes, leaving the infant's eyes scarred. The "doctor" left town—and Fanny blind.

Growing up blind wasn't easy, but Fanny didn't blame God for her situation. She didn't ask, "Why me?" Instead, she determined in her heart to make a difference in this world. She expressed that desire in her first poem:

O what a happy soul am I!
Although I cannot see,
I am resolved that in this world,
Contented I will be.
How many blessings I enjoy,
That other people don't.

To weep and sigh because I'm blind,
I cannot and I won't!

When adversity happens in life, people respond in different ways. Some give up. Some get angry with God. And some become even more determined to reach their goals and dreams—like Fanny. Without her songs "Safe in the Arms of Jesus," "Pass Me Not, O Gentle Savior," "Blessed Assurance," and so many others, our world would not be the same.

So here's my question to you: What are you letting hold you back? If you've been dealing with a painful disability or if you've been emotionally crippled due to circumstances beyond your control, God cares. He knows you're hurting. But He wants to give you beauty for ashes. He wants you to know that His plans for you have been in existence since before the foundations of the earth. Despite your troubles, God's plan for you has never changed, and His plan is a good one!

If you don't know the plan that God has for you, ask Him to show you. Tell Him that you are ready to carry out all that He has for you to do. Like Fanny, you are an important part of His overall plan in this world. So go ahead. Walk in that plan.

BECOMING BEAUTIFULLY OBEDIENT

*"If you love me,
show it by doing what I've told you."*
JOHN 14:15 MSG

Mary, mother of Jesus, is the most well-known woman in the Bible. We all know the facts about her. Mary was from the line of King David. She was very young when she became engaged to Joseph. We also know that when the angel of the Lord came to Mary and told her that she would become pregnant, she asked, "How can this be? I am a virgin." After the angel of the Lord explained how the Holy Spirit could come upon her and make her pregnant, Mary never doubted or questioned anything else. Instead, Mary responded, "I am the Lord's servant, and I am willing to accept whatever he wants. May everything you have said come true."

Wow. That totally amazes me. Mary didn't say, "Well, Mr. Angel, I think that's great, but I am engaged and my future husband is not going to understand or believe this whole story about my pregnancy, so maybe this isn't such a good idea." No, Mary rejoiced over the news. She didn't worry about herself. She didn't care what others thought. She just wanted to be obedient to her God.

For years, Bible historians have asked the question: Why did God choose Mary to carry His Son? Why her? Maybe God chose Mary because she had such an obedient heart. The Bible says that man looks on the outward appearance while God looks on the heart. See, God knew that Mary would do all that He needed her to do. He knew that she loved Him that much. God saw Mary's beautiful, obedient heart and knew she would be the perfect woman to bring Jesus into the world.

I want to be more like Mary, don't you? I want God to trust me so much that He chooses me for assignments because He knows that I'll be obedient. I want my heart to be so beautiful before God that He can't wait to use me.

Obedience really is a beautiful thing. Conversely, disobedience is quite unattractive to God. Even delayed obedience is disobedience. God wants us to trust Him so much that when He asks us to do something, we do it—flat out. No questions. No wondering. No delayed response. Just obedience.

If you are struggling with obedience today, ask God to help you. Tell Him that you long to be His go-to gal. Determine to be obedient in the little things, and soon your heart will be beautifully obedient before God. And like Mary, you'll get big assignments, too!

A LITTLE R & R

*The LORD replied,
"My Presence will go with you,
and I will give you rest."*

EXODUS 33:14 NIV

Rise before daylight, spend a few minutes with God, get the kids up for school, pack their lunches, slurp down a glass of OJ while showering, get dressed, brush your teeth, make sure the kids get on the bus, put on a little mascara, do the nine-to-five thing, pick up the dry cleaning, go to the grocery store, rush home and fix dinner, help the kids with their homework, do a load of laundry, have at least one meaningful conversation with your husband, look over your notes for tomorrow's meeting, call your mother, watch the eleven o'clock news, and collapse into bed.

Sound familiar?

If you're like most women, you only know one speed—full speed ahead! There have been seasons in my life when I just wanted to "jump ship" and swim for shore. Bottom line—we're too busy today.

God didn't intend for us to be so busy. Psalm 23:1–3 (NLT) says: "The LORD is my shepherd; I have everything I need. He lets me rest in green meadows; he leads me beside peaceful streams. He renews my strength."

So how long has it been since you've rested in green meadows? My guess is—too long! Pastor

Joel Osteen of Lakewood Church in Houston, Texas, says that he has to have a few minutes in his recliner each day to simply meditate on the goodness of God. Without those minutes of just sitting before God, he feels out of balance.

Pastor Osteen is not alone. If we don't take time to just sit before God and meditate on His goodness and His promises, we might spin our wheels all day long. But you say, "Michelle, I have my daily devotional time each morning. I read one chapter of the Bible and a devotional entry, and pray for fifteen minutes. I'm doing fine!" My response is this: You are doing well! Those things are very important, but if your prayer life is like mine, you spend all fifteen minutes praying for everyone on your prayer list, thank God for loving you, and call it good. You rarely just sit in His presence and rest in Him.

We need that green meadow time. Make a conscious decision today to rest in Him. Find a few minutes to bask in His glory. Pencil in "green meadow" time in your daily planner and stick to it. God is waiting.

BE A LOVE POWER WALKER!

The most important piece of clothing you must wear is love. Love is what binds us all together in perfect harmony.

COLOSSIANS 3:14 NLT

There's nothing more attractive than love. I recently heard a pastor say, "Love leads people to Christ, not preaching." Wow. I never thought of it that way before, but it's really true. People today are so hungry for love, they're looking for it. And if you have the love of Jesus to offer, they'll want it!

Listen, sister chick, if your husband is not currently serving God, this is for you. He will be won over to Christ through your loving spirit, not your nagging nature. So if you're spending all of your time preaching at him, telling him that he needs to get his sorry self to church, that's not showing him love.

Instead of running all over town to every Bible study going, spend some quality time with your husband, loving him and respecting him. You don't have to honor the sin in his life; you just have to honor him. Call things that are not as though they were—call your husband a wonderful man of God. Speak your desired result. Put on his favorite perfume and a little lip gloss, and give him a kiss on the neck. Speak sweetly to him. Love him. And watch him come around. Before long, he will be sitting next to you in the pew. How do I know this? Because the Word tells us that love never fails.

Love changes the atmosphere. So if your love-walk is more of a love-crawl these days, you need to take a crash course. Here's your assignment: Read 1 Corinthians 13 every single day. Meditate on the different aspects of love, such as: "Love is patient. Love is kind. It does not envy. It does not boast. It is not proud," and ask God to develop each of those attributes in you.

Look for opportunities to share love with everyone around you—especially your spouse. Pretty soon, you'll be a love power walker, sharing the love of Jesus with your family, friends, and a world that so desperately needs it. The more you walk in love, the higher your love-fitness level will become! Your love will make the God in you so attractive, people will be curious about you. They'll want to know what makes you different—what makes you stand out in a crowd. And you can share the answer—Jesus! Just as you should never step out without putting on your lipstick, you should never step out without love.

THE SKINNY WARS AND OTHER SILLY COMPETITIONS

We won't dare compare ourselves with those who think so much of themselves. But they are foolish to compare themselves with themselves.

2 CORINTHIANS 10:12 CEV

I recently read an article about "The Skinny Wars" going on in Hollywood. It seems that female stars who appear on the same show are competing (either consciously or subconsciously) to see who can lose the most weight. To illustrate this Hollywood trend, the magazine showed pictures of Jennifer Aniston and Courtney Cox when they first began *Friends* in 1994 and how they looked a decade later. It was unbelievable. They'd shrunk three or four sizes. They had dropped from the 130s to 105 or so. To further drive home the point, they showed how the already skinny starlets from *Ally McBeal* dwindled down to almost nothing before the series ended.

So are you in a skinny war, too? Maybe you're not trying to lose more weight than your female buddies, but are you competing against them in other ways? I'll admit, I am very competitive by nature, so I really struggle with this one. Chances are, you do, too. Women tend to get caught up in comparing and competing, and it never turns out well.

Competition can be healthy if it pushes you to do better in an area of your life, but if you're consumed with being better than someone else, that's not healthy. That's a wrong focus. You need to get your eyes off of that person and back on Jesus. The Word tells us that we are to fix our eyes on Jesus. See, if our eyes are fixed on Jesus, we won't be distracted by competition and unhealthy comparisons. Rather, we'll be focused on becoming more like Him, and that's a worthy goal.

Remember that God has a race all mapped out for you. You can't run somebody else's race. It won't ever feel right, and it won't bring you joy even if you win. You have to run the race that God has for you. It's your destiny. Don't waste time on the "skinny wars" of this world. Instead, focus on Jesus. You'll always be a winner if you do that!

Experiencing Happily Ever After

So put on all the armor that God gives. Then when that evil day comes, you will be able to defend yourself. And when the battle is over, you will still be standing firm.

Ephesians 6:13 CEV

I love fairy tales. My daughters love fairy tales, too. Even the offbeat ones like *Shrek*. Have you ever noticed that in a fairy tale there's usually a damsel in distress? Typically, there is a beautiful princess who is held captive in a tower that is surrounded by a moat full of alligators and the occasional fire-breathing dragon. She waits in that tower, hoping that someday her prince will come. She dreams about the day a valiant knight on his white horse will ride up to the castle, slay the dragon, use the alligators as stepping-stones, climb up the tower, and rescue her.

Maybe you've had that dream yourself. Well, stop dreaming, sister! Your dream has already come true, and it's heavenly! Your Prince (the Prince of Peace) has already come on His white horse. He rescued you from that tower of sin more than two thousand years ago. And He didn't just rescue you. He also took away your victim status and made you into a victor! He turned you into an overcomer. He even gave you armor—the full armor of God—to protect you as you fight evil and rescue others from that fire-breathing dragon—aka Satan.

Sure, fairy tales are fun to watch on the big screen, but I don't want to be a damsel in distress in real life. A princess—yes. A damsel in distress—no. God doesn't want you to be a damsel in distress, either. If you've been living with a victim's mentality for too long, it's time to wise up to the Word. God says that you are more than a conqueror through Christ Jesus. His Word says that you are highly favored. It says that God did not give you a spirit of fear. The Word says that we can use God's mighty weapons to knock down the devil's strongholds. Like evangelist Jesse Duplantis always says, "I read the back of the Book, and we win!"

Your damsel-in-distress days are behind you. You are a winner. You are a beautiful princess—a member of God's royal family. In *Beauty and the Beast*, you get to be Beauty. In *Cinderella*, you get to be the lovely Cinderella. In *Shrek*, you get to be. . .er, uh, Princess Fiona (when she isn't an ogre). And if you've made Jesus the Lord of your life, you are promised an eternity of "happily ever after." Now that's a story worth sharing!

BULLDOG FAITH

*And he did not do many miracles there
because of their lack of faith.*

MATTHEW 13:58 NIV

Have you ever heard the theory that people end up owning the dog breed that they most resemble in the looks department? Well, I'd have to say that is true when it comes to me. I am the proud "mama" to three long-haired miniature dachshunds. They have long noses and very short legs. Yeah, I would have to say that I share those same figure flaws. (You're checking out your dog right now, aren't you?)

But in the spiritual realm, we all need to resemble English bulldogs. Bible teacher Kate McVeigh once shared that Christians need to have bulldog faith. She said, "A bulldog only knows one thing. That bone is his, and he's taking it." And that bulldog won't let loose of that bone—no matter what. In fact, the English bulldog's jaw muscles are as strong as any athlete's muscle, and when it latches on to something, it really latches on.

Well, guess what? That's how we have to be when it comes to our faith. In Mark 11:23–24 (NIV), Jesus says, "I tell you the truth, if anyone says to this mountain, 'Go, throw yourself into the sea,' and does not doubt in his heart but believes that what he says will happen, it will be done for him. Therefore I tell you, whatever you ask for in prayer, believe that you have received it, and it will be yours."

In other words, you have to believe you have received your deliverance from drugs. You have to believe you have received your healing. You have to believe you've received a restored marriage. You have to believe that you've received your dream job. And then you can't be moved if it doesn't happen overnight. You have to get a locked jaw of faith on whatever it is you're trusting God to do in your life, and you can't turn loose until the desired result comes. So go ahead. Growl in the face of adversity and develop that bulldog faith. It may be a dog-eat-dog world out there, but with bulldog faith, you'll have a beautiful existence.

UNCONDITIONAL LOVE

And now these three remain:
faith, hope and love.
But the greatest of these is love.

1 CORINTHIANS 13:13 NIV

Do you love your family unconditionally? How about your friends? How about your coworkers? Okay, now for the tough question. You know that woman at church who gets on your very last nerve—do you love her unconditionally?

According to Colossians 2:2 (NKJV), as Christians our hearts are supposed to be knit together in love—agape love. Agape doesn't mean "I'll love you if. . ." Agape means "I'll love you regardless." That's the same way that God loves us—in spite of all our flaws. We are to follow His example and love others unconditionally, too.

But agape love isn't an easy kind of love. It's the kind of love you have to work at all the time. That means you have to love your spouse even when he acts unlovely to you. That means you have to love your coworker even when she takes credit for something you've done. That means you have to love your teenager when he screams, "I hate you!" That means you have to love yourself even though your past is dotted with shameful events. You have to love all people all the time.

Sure, there will be times when everything

in you will want to act less than lovely toward someone who has hurt you, but practice love anyway. When you release agape love into a situation, it's like releasing God. Talk about powerful! Once you begin practicing love, you'll become totally consumed with it. Pretty soon, love will be your first instinct.

Bible teacher Billye Brim practices love in that manner. She once shared through tears how upset she was when a person verbally attacked her. But Billye wasn't upset about what was said to her. Instead, she was upset that those remarks had actually offended her, because that meant she wasn't walking in agape love. That's the kind of love-walk I desire. How about you?

Well, I've got good news. It's not out of our reach. Jesus wouldn't have commanded us to love one another if we weren't capable of doing so. Ask Him to fill you with agape love today. Make a decision to show unconditional love to everyone you encounter. Pretty soon, the world will look a lot better to you, and you'll look a lot better to everyone in your world.

FOLLOW THE DIRECTIONS—EXACTLY!

Now if you will faithfully obey me, you will be my very own people. The whole world is mine.

EXODUS 19:5 CEV

Recently, talk show queen Oprah Winfrey revealed that she lives in shaper panties. She shared that clothes just look better over them, pointing out that spandex shaper undergarments hold everything in its place without any visible panty lines. *Well,* I thought, *that sounds good to me.* I went on a quest to buy the specific brand of shaper undies that Oprah mentioned on her show, but apparently every other woman in America did the same thing. They were sold out! So I settled for a different brand that promised to deliver the exact same results.

They are probably all the same, I figured, *so I'll just make do with this off-brand.*

Big mistake!

The shaper panties I bought had some weird spandex around the upper thigh that made the leg part of the panties bulge out. That's a nice look—bulging fat spilling forth beneath spandex leg bands. It was disastrous. And what's worse, I couldn't return them because they were underwear! So now I dust the house with my shaper panties. (At least I found something they are good for!) My problem? I didn't follow Oprah's exact directions. I didn't buy the shaper undies she recommended. I bought an off-brand, and the results were *so* not good.

You know, it's the same way with God. If you don't follow His exact directions, the results are never as good as they could have been, and sometimes they're disastrous. If you know in your heart that God has told you to volunteer for the Sunday school superintendent position at your church but you'd rather be in charge of the Christmas musical because there's a lot more glory associated with it—watch out. I see bad spiritual panty lines in your future!

If you go ahead and disregard the Holy Spirit's leading and take on the Christmas musical, it will probably be one of the hardest tasks you've ever done. See, God doesn't want our sacrifice; He wants our obedience.

Walking in obedience to God is much more than just obeying the Ten Commandments. It's about listening to His leading and following His exact directions. If you miss God once in a while but your heart is right, don't worry. God will find you. But make a decision today to walk in obedience. If you do, you'll be in good shape—no matter what you wear!

GIVE IT TO GOD

"If you, then, though you are evil,
know how to give good gifts to your children,
how much more will your Father in heaven
give good gifts to those who ask him!"

MATTHEW 7:11 NIV

I love happy endings, don't you? That's why I love the story of Hannah in the Bible. Hannah was a good wife to Elkanah, but she couldn't bear any children. Back then, that was the worst possible thing that could happen to a woman. In fact, a childless woman was often divorced, or another wife was added to fulfill the childbearing duties. Either way, the barren wife lived a bitter existence. Well, this is what poor Hannah faced.

Even though Elkanah told Hannah that she was his best-loved wife, Peninnah was the wife having all the babies. And to make matters worse, Peninnah constantly taunted Hannah about her inability to conceive. Can't you just imagine the tension in that household?

Hannah became quite depressed over the situation, and she prayed earnestly to God for a child of her own. Then she promised God that if He gave her a son, she would consecrate him to the Lord's service all of his life. God heard her prayer and she became pregnant with Samuel. You can imagine her delight. I bet she strutted her pregnant self in front of Peninnah every chance she got, don't you? But then it came time to follow through on her vow to God. After raising her only baby for several years, nursing him and loving him, she delivered Samuel to the house of the Lord, turning him over to Eli the priest. Hannah followed through and honored God because He had honored her. Don't you imagine that her heart ached as she journeyed home without her son?

But see, you can never outdo God. He loves to give blessings to His children. So God caused Hannah to become pregnant with several more children. She was no longer the barren wife of the house. God had changed all of that. God turned her unhappy life into a lovely situation.

We can learn much from Hannah's beautiful heart. She didn't take matters into her own hands and throttle Peninnah, although her flesh probably wanted to do just that. Instead, she cried out to God and trusted Him to meet her needs. That blesses God. He loves it when we come to Him as our Abba Father and say, "Daddy, we can't change this situation, but we know that You can. So we're trusting You to do so." And He will. Whatever you're struggling with today—give it to God. He has a beautiful happy ending waiting just for you!

LET YOUR LIGHT SHINE

*"You're here to be light, bringing
out the God-colors in the world.
God is not a secret to be kept.
We're going public with this,
as public as a city on a hill."*

MATTHEW 5:14 MSG

Mary and her husband, Danny, own and operate the Bedford Bible Bookstore in Bedford, Indiana. It is the place to go if you need a wonderful gift item, VBS prizes for the kiddos, the latest Christian music, or just about any inspirational book you can imagine. If Mary doesn't have it, she can get it for you.

The Bedford Bible Bookstore has stood the test of time. Sure, there's a Barnes & Noble store thirty minutes up the road, but there's no Mary at Barnes & Noble. See, Mary doesn't just sell you products. She listens to your concerns. She celebrates with you over answered prayers. She points you toward the book that holds information you've been seeking. She also offers hugs. Mary makes a difference.

In fact, would you believe the Bedford Bible Bookstore has sold more copies of *The Power of a Praying Wife* by Stormie Omartian than any other Christian bookstore in the five states that her sales representative services? And compared to many of those bookstores, Danny and Mary's bookstore is much smaller. You see, that book so touched Mary's heart that she has shared it with thousands of women who have passed through the doors of the Bedford Bible Bookstore. Just think how many marriages have been enriched and possibly even saved because Mary pointed them toward Stormie's book. You might say Mary is letting her little light shine.

Mary may never know how many lives she's touched until she gets to heaven, but her willingness to let God use her has made a difference in thousands of lives. I know because I am one of them. So here's my question to you: Are you letting your little light shine in your corner of the world? Mary didn't have to go to Africa to let her light shine. God is using her on her own mission field—Bedford, Indiana. Why not let your light shine where you live? You can make a big difference with your little light. So go ahead. Let it shine!

WHAT'S YOUR TRADEMARK?

*Take on an entirely new way of life—
a God-fashioned life, a life renewed from the
inside and working itself into your conduct as
God accurately reproduces his character in you.*

EPHESIANS 4:23–24 MSG

Do you have a signature piece of jewelry that you wear all the time? Maybe an estate piece that's been in the family for a long time. Or how about a certain perfume? Some women wear a "signature fragrance" that really expresses who they are. My mother-in-law, Martha, has worn Clinique Aromatics Elixir for years. Every time I smell it somewhere, I think of her because that's her signature fragrance.

I've never really had a signature anything. I pretty much just flow in and out of whatever is "hot" this week and totally "not in" the next. That doesn't leave much time to establish a trademark anything. But this past spring I treated myself to a Mother's Day present—from me to me. (Those are the best kind of gifts, don't you think? You always ensure you get a gift, and you're guaranteed to get what you want.) I bought myself a Tiffany & Co. sterling silver necklace with a matching bracelet. I absolutely love it. It seems that almost every day I reach for it. That set goes with most every outfit. Even though I love it, I don't necessarily want to be *known* for it. I'd much rather be known for my Christian walk. How about you?

If we are truly living for the Lord, we should

have a special way about us—something totally different from the world. We should have the fruits of the Spirit—love, joy, peace, patience, kindness, goodness, faithfulness, gentleness, and self-control—operating in our lives at such a level that people notice them. We should walk in such favor that folks expect for things to go our way. You might say we should wear our "Signature Jesus" every single day.

Just think—you might be the only glimpse of Jesus that some people ever see, so make sure you don't leave home without your Signature Jesus. Wear Him proudly—He's even better than Versace! He goes with everything. He's always in style. And He wants you to share Him with the world. In fact, He commanded it. So go ahead. Let the world see the Jesus in you! Soon, you'll become known for Him, and that's not only fashionable, that's scriptural.

SEEING SPOTS

If we confess our sins to him,
he is faithful and just to forgive us
and to cleanse us from every wrong.

1 JOHN 1:9 NLT

R emember the old exercise videos in which Jane Fonda would make you do a million buttocks lifts and then say, "Now, go for the burn"? Yeah, me, too. Then we progressed to "Buns of Steel," "Abs of Steel," and any other body part of steel we could find. And how could we forget the "Thighmaster" contraption? (I still like this one!)

Spot reducing has been around for a very long time. There's just one problem with spot reducing—it doesn't work all by itself. In other words, if you tighten and tone the muscles in your bum, but there is still a whole lot of fat on top of that muscle, you're not going to see the results you desire. That's why spot reducing never produces the results you want if you don't also partake in some sort of cardio activity to burn the fat. Think of it this way—if you have a six-pack for abs but you have six inches of fat on top of the abdominal muscles, no one will ever know you have a toned tummy.

Spot reducing in the spiritual realm doesn't work that well, either. If you work on your anger problem but you leave those six inches of unforgiveness untouched, it won't really make a difference. Or if you work hard memorizing scriptures in order to build your faith but you still have a layer of sin covering your heart, it's just a memorization activity.

Here's the good news. In the spiritual realm, you don't have to do cardio to get rid of those layers of sin. It's much easier. All you have to do is confess your sins and ask God to forgive you. The Word says He will! Then He will help you "spot reduce" until your spiritual life is as fit as Fonda. You don't have to go for the burn. You just have to go to God!

The Innocence of Youth

*Don't let anyone look down on you because
you are young, but set an example for
the believers in speech, in life,
in love, in faith and in purity.*

1 Timothy 4:12 NIV

Hannah is our sweet little neighbor. She may be only eight years old in the natural, but she is much older and wiser spiritually speaking. In fact, she's my role model. This is the last week of school here in Texas, and Hannah's second grade class had its award ceremony yesterday.

Hannah is a very smart little girl, too. She won ribbons for making the straight-A honor roll, A's all year, an accelerated reader ribbon, and several other awards, too. Hannah had worked hard to earn each one of those ribbons. She was proud of them. She was very happy—until she saw her best friend's sadness. See, Hannah's little friend hadn't earned as many ribbons, and she was pretty upset. Hannah gave her friend a big hug and said, "It's okay. You can have one of mine." With that, Hannah handed her friend the accelerated reader ribbon.

Hannah's mom, Stephanie, told me later, "I was proud of Hannah for earning all of those academic ribbons, but nothing could've made me happier than when Hannah gave her reading ribbon to her friend." It was a selfless, loving act, and Hannah didn't think twice about doing it.

If only we could all be more like Hannah.

As children, we still believe the best in others. We still root for the underdog. We still care about others' feelings. But as we get older, we become jaded. We start acquiring that emotional baggage. We feel we must look out for number one or we'll never get ahead. Maybe that's why Jesus said the kingdom of heaven belongs to the children (Matthew 19:14).

Maybe it's time for you to get in touch with your inner child—the one who still believes the best in people. The one who has no emotional baggage. . .the one who isn't worried about number one. . .the one who gives up a prized possession just to make a friend feel better—the one who acts like Jesus. We all want to look younger, but we should all want to act younger, too! Follow Hannah's lead and become childlike today.

EXPERT OPINIONS—
NO THANKS!

*Then I heard a loud voice saying in heaven,
"Now salvation, and strength,
and the kingdom of our God,
and the power of His Christ have come,
for the accuser of our brethren,
who accused them before our God
day and night, has been cast down."*

REVELATION 12:10 NKJV

Actress Debra Messing, who is known for her beauty, shared that she was always a little self-conscious about her looks, but after she became famous and sat in a makeup artist's chair every day, she said she learned she had more flaws than she'd ever realized. "The experts" were quick to point out her flaws and what they'd have to do to make her appear flawless. Talk about scary!

It's kind of like *Ambush Makeover* on Fox. Have you ever seen that show? You leave the house thinking you look pretty good, then suddenly you're ambushed by "an expert" who begins telling you that your hair is frizzy, your makeup is all wrong, and you look stupid in your ripped jeans. Ugh! *Please* don't sign me up for that show. (I think I'll go with the ignorance is bliss approach on this one!)

There's one thing for sure: The world is full of "experts" who will happily point out your flaws—even if you don't ask for their expert opinions. Sometimes those experts are in your family. You go to the annual family picnic and your aunt Lucy says, "Ooh, you've put on a lot of weight since last year. I read where you should drink more water to lose weight fast—can I get you a bottle of water, dear?" Or your best friend says, "I recently read about a new wrinkle cream that is guaranteed to diminish crow's-feet. I cut out the ad for you." Nice, huh? Oh, yes, we love those expert opinions.

Yep, experts lurk around every corner. The devil even fancies himself as an expert. He loves to point out all of your flaws. The Bible says that he is an accuser of the brethren. In other words, he loves to tell you what a crudball you are because if he can convince you that you're a crudball, he knows you'll never live out the beautiful life that God has planned for you. Like most of these so-called experts, the devil's opinion is worth about as much as the gum on the bottom of your shoe. Ignore him! You may not be perfect, but you're perfectly saved. You're perfectly loved by God. And if you've asked Jesus to be your Lord and Savior, your heart is flawless. So take that, devil! We're hot! And you just live where it's hot.

MEASURING UP—
EVEN IN THE MORNING

For we are his workmanship,
created in Christ Jesus for good works.

EPHESIANS 2:10 ASV

D o you remember the first time your significant other saw you looking less than lovely? I sure do. Jeff and I were high school sweethearts, so he had only seen me at school and on weekends when I looked my best. Then I became really ill and had to check into the local hospital. Jeff and I had only been dating about four months when all of this happened. Of course, he came to visit me in the hospital, bearing balloons and flowers. And though I wanted to put on a little lip gloss, I was too weak. I looked like death warmed over when he came to see me. I remember thinking, *Well, if he still likes me after seeing me that way, it must be love.* As it turns out, it was love!

But that was scary. I was so nervous for him to see me "all natural," with every flaw exposed. Apparently, I'm not alone. In a recent report featured on the www.healthzone.co.uk Web site, one in five women said her biggest fear about traveling with her boyfriend for the holidays was letting him see her looking less than lovely in the morning. Women said they were afraid to lose that air of mystery they'd worked so hard to create.

Why are we so afraid of letting down our

guards? For many women, it comes down to one thing—we're afraid we won't measure up. Even legendary film stars and Hollywood hotties struggle with self-esteem issues. I recently heard gorgeous actress Cameron Diaz comment about her new reality show, "Trippin'," in which she nervously joked, "Oh, the pimples." The camera caught everything in film—even the less-than-perfect skin that Cameron was sporting in several of the episodes. See, even a "Charlie's Angel" gets a zit once in a while! We can't be glamorous all of the time.

So, aren't you glad that God loves us for who we are—the good, the bad, and the ugly? We can totally be ourselves with God. He knows us inside and out—after all, He made us! The Father sees you through eyes of love, and He thinks you're beautiful. You don't have to worry about impressing God. He already thinks you're great—even when you first get up in the morning. Now that's real love!

JUST WHEN YOU THINK YOU'VE ARRIVED...

I don't mean to say that I have already achieved these things or that I have already reached perfection! But I keep working toward that day when I will finally be all that Christ Jesus saved me for and wants me to be.

PHILIPPIANS 3:12 NLT

After my father died, I did a bit of emotional eating. Okay, I did a lot of emotional eating, which resulted in some weight gain. So I turned to LA Weight Loss to help me gain control of my eating. I had to relearn how to eat. After four months, I lost those ten pounds plus another five—for a whopping fifteen-pound weight loss. I was thrilled, and so were my weight-loss counselors. Once I hit my weight-loss goal, I was put on the maintenance program, which was a lot less restrictive than the original program. I loved it! But I loved it a bit too much. I developed a false sense of security and, little by little, those pounds found their way back onto my scale. After about six pounds, I put myself back on the restrictive program and lost those pounds again. I had learned a lesson—don't get too confident or thrilled with what you've accomplished. Keep your eye on the goal. (Oh, and don't keep mini Snickers bars in your purse.)

This same principle operates in the spiritual realm. I recently heard Bible teacher and TV host Paula White say, "If you ever think you've arrived spiritually, you're already in trouble." In other words, there's always more. There's always a deeper place with God. There's always more to learn from the Bible.

Maybe that's why the Word says that pride comes before a fall. If you ever think you've arrived spiritually and quit pressing toward the goal, the devil is there to jerk that rug out from underneath your little feet. After that happens, the fall is sure to come. See, the enemy has only one goal—to kill, steal, and destroy. So if he sees an opening, he's taking it. Don't give him that opening. Don't be fooled into a false sense of security. If the apostle Paul felt that he needed to keep pressing on, I'm sure that all of us have some more spiritual growing to do.

Never be satisfied with your walk with God. Keep desiring more of Him. Keep learning more from His Word. Listen to more teaching tapes. Spend more time meditating on His promises. Keep your eyes fixed on Jesus. Press on! You have much to gain, and it won't be weight.

BE COURAGEOUS!

*Jesus turned. He saw the woman and said,
"Don't worry! You are now well because of
your faith." At that moment she was healed.*
MATTHEW 9:22 CEV

It takes courage to launch a new fitness and diet plan. The fear of failure—again—keeps many would-be exercisers and dieters from embarking on the journey toward a better way of life. Even though they know they'll look and feel better if they do begin such programs, they just can't muster enough courage to try. Fear is a powerful emotion that holds many people in bondage—whether that bondage is weight, drugs, debt, or something else.

The definition of courage, according to one source on Dictionary.com, is "a quality of spirit that enables you to face danger of pain without showing fear." The Bible is full of examples of courage, such as the woman with the issue of blood. She was in a tough situation.

This woman had been sick for more than a decade. The Bible tells us that she'd spent all of her money on doctors, and yet she still wasn't well. She was sick and poor. And because she was suffering with a bleeding problem, she was deemed "unclean." So she was also a social outcast on top of being sick and poor. Talk about desperate! This woman knew she needed a miracle, and she was determined to get one.

No doubt she had heard of Jesus and His

miracle-working power. She knew in her heart that if she could only touch Him, she'd receive her total healing. Yet, as an unclean woman, she wasn't supposed to be out in public. She knew if she were found out she could be killed. Still, she had to try. So she pushed her way through the mass of humanity. Trying to go unnoticed, she reached out and touched the hem of Jesus' garment. At that moment, Jesus stopped and asked, "Who touched me?" The woman knew He meant her and fessed up. That final courageous act changed her life forever. Jesus said, "Don't worry. You are now well because of your faith."

If she hadn't taken a risk and overcome her fear, she wouldn't have been made whole. So what are you afraid of? Failure? Success? Rejection? What is keeping you in bondage? The Word says we do not have a spirit of fear. The Bible also says we can do all things through Christ, who gives us strength. So whatever is holding you back, break free! If you need to lose weight, be courageous. Your miracle is at hand!

KNOWLEDGE IS POWER

*My people are ruined because they
don't know what's right or true.*

HOSEA 4:6 MSG

Q. What do you call it when a blond dyes her hair brunette?

A. Artificial intelligence.

Entire Web sites are dedicated to dumb-blond jokes. Even though I'm not a natural blond (There, I said it!), I take blond jokes quite personally. No one wants to be thought of as an airhead or a clueless person. That's definitely not attractive. While it's fun to watch dumb blonds in movies and television sitcoms, in real life being dumb (whether you're blond, redheaded, or brunette) is not a laughing matter.

Oh, sure, we all have our clueless moments from time to time. When you get older, they call them "senior moments." I guess before you qualify for senior discounts, they are called "blond moments." Whatever you want to call them, they happen. Most of the time they are harmless—like locking your keys in the car or momentarily forgetting the name of a friend or associate. These are simple lapses in memory—not a lack of knowledge. There's a difference.

The Old Testament prophet Hosea wrote that God's people were being destroyed by a lack of knowledge. In other words, what you don't know *will* hurt you. That's why we need to know God's Word. We need to understand our promises and covenant rights and walk in them every single day. God created us and then left us an owner's manual—the Bible. It's a road map for life. In it you'll discover the paths that lead to health, wholeness, peace, renewed strength, and a beautiful life. But if we don't take time to read it and memorize it and meditate on its words, then we will lack knowledge. Maybe that lack of knowledge won't cause physical death, but it might cause the death of a relationship or the loss of a job.

The world has taken this biblical principle and created the slogan "Knowledge is power." Maybe you've heard it before. Well, that's really true. When you have knowledge of God's Word, you will be empowered. Even your "blond moments" will be fewer and farther between. Wisdom is a beautiful thing, and there is wisdom in the Word—so get it!

Don't Be Moved!

By the grace given me I say to every one of you:
Do not think of yourself more highly than
you ought, but rather think of yourself with
sober judgment, in accordance with the
measure of faith God has given you.

Romans 12:3 NIV

Singer and actress Britney Spears was voted the sexiest woman in the world by a popular men's magazine in 2004. But in 2005, Spears didn't even make the Top 100 list! She went from being number one to disappearing from the list in one year. Did Spears suddenly lose her sex appeal? Did she lose her loveliness? No, on both counts. As it turns out, the only explanation is this—the world is fickle. People will love you one moment and passionately praise you, and the next moment they may lynch you. Crazy, isn't it?

That's why you can't be moved by what everyone else thinks. This is especially true when it comes to your outward appearance. One day you may get fifteen compliments on your new haircut, and the next day you'll get a zinger something like this: "Wow, you got your hair cut, huh? Don't worry. I had a bad haircut once. It will grow. Lucky for you, hats are in again this season."

Praise is a funny thing. While it's nice to receive, it can also destroy you if you let it deceive you into thinking too highly of yourself. Beautiful actress, television personality, and singer Jessica Simpson was recently quoted in a *Glamour* cover story as saying: "In this business, you're surrounded by people who praise you all day long. Even at the photo shoot for this cover people kept saying, 'You look so hot.' It's easy to turn into a diva and lose the qualities that made people like you in the first place. And I don't ever want to become that." (Pretty wise words from a person who didn't know if buffalo wings were chicken or if they really came from buffalo!)

So if you rely too heavily on what others think of you—especially what they think of your appearance—you'll never be consistently happy. People change. Their opinions change. But God never changes. He is the same yesterday, today, and forever. And He always thinks you're lovely. After all, He created you in His very likeness. It's like that old expression says, "God made me, and He doesn't make any junk." Hallelujah! Get in the Word of God and discover how God views you. Talk about a self-esteem boost! He adores you, and He always has—even when you wore the "mullet" back in the 1980s.

Don't be moved by praise or criticism. Just go to God and find your identity in Him.

BE THE GLUE

A woman's family is held together by her wisdom,
but it can be destroyed by her foolishness.

PROVERBS 14:1 CEV

Remember the old television commercial for Super Glue featuring the construction worker? The man puts glue on the top of his hard hat and glues himself to a beam. Before the commercial is through, you see that construction worker holding on to his hat, his feet dangling beneath him, several feet off the ground. Of course, the goal of this commercial is to make you think, "Wow, that glue is really strong—maybe I should buy some of that."

Super Glue is really strong stuff. I have mistakenly glued my thumb and index finger together, and, wow, was it tough to separate them! (Yes, that was one of those blond moments we talked about a bit earlier.) Here's my challenge to you today: Become like Super Glue for your family.

That may seem like a strange goal to you, but it's a worthy one. You should have God so big on the inside of you that His beautiful love, gorgeous goodness, and attractive acceptance emanate from you onto your family—sticking them together. In today's world, it's tough to keep a family intact. Divorce, even in the Christian community, is at an all-time high. Children run away from home. Family members turn their backs on one another. Let's face it: The Christian family is under attack. That's why it's so important to become the glue for your family.

So how do you become the Super Glue for your family? Live out the love of Jesus in your home. Let your family see your faith. Pray for each family member every single day. Speak peace over your household. Let God bond your family together with His supreme love, and get ready to experience a beautiful home life. Pretty soon, others will ask how you "keep it all together." They'll want to know why your family is different. And you'll be able to tell them about God's love and His peace and His goodness. Your words will stick in their minds, and pretty soon they'll be the glue for their families!

Sticking it out—especially when times are tough—is rare in today's world. But as Christians, we should set the example for a beautiful, happy home life. So be the glue today!

LOOKING FOR A MIRACLE

You are the God who performs miracles;
you display your power among the peoples.
PSALM 77:14 NIV

I love to read beauty magazines. From *Glamour* to *Shape*, I read them all. But you know what I love reading even more than the wonderfully written articles? The advertisements. So many times you'll see ads saying things like, "Lose 30 pounds in 30 days!" or "Face-lift in a bottle." Oh, yeah, bring on the miracle-working products, right? We are hungry for miracles. We crave products that really work as much as we crave dark chocolate. We long to encounter something that brings results—not just in our beauty routines but also in our spiritual lives.

This week I saw the most amazing phenomenon on the evening news. A woman looked out her apartment window and believed she saw the face of Jesus forming on the glass. "If you look closely," she said, "you can see the outline of His face and hair. I saw it forming! I couldn't believe it!"

Word of the image soon spread throughout the area, and hundreds of cars started lining up in front of her home—just to catch a glimpse of the "Window Jesus." People began crying and worshiping God right there in the front of a window. Why? Because people are hungry for a miracle. They are so hungry for a touch from God, they'll wait in line for hours in hopes of seeing the outline of Jesus' face on an apartment window.

Let me ask you something. How hungry are you for God? Do you crave His presence in your life? Or have you lost that passion for Him? If Jesus is no longer the first love in your life, spend some quality time with Him and His Word today. Ask Him to become first place in your life again, and thank Him for restoring that love on the inside of you.

Then determine to be the "Window Jesus" for others. If people are so hungry for the supernatural, miracle-working power of God—offer it to them! Don't be shy. They crave it! When you see someone crying in the supermarket, offer to pray with that person. Let Jesus shine through you. Be that window for Him. The world is hungry for what you have, so why not share it today? The world would be a lot more beautiful if we let His light shine through us everywhere we went. So shine on, and let the miracle-working love of Jesus flow out of you today!

RESISTANCE ROCKS!

*My brethren, count it all joy when you fall
into various trials, knowing that the
testing of your faith produces patience.*

JAMES 1:2–3 NKJV

Resistance training brings results. I learned this when I first started doing some personal training back in the early nineties. I had always thought that lifting weights was reserved for the grunting, sweaty, bodybuilding kind of guys. I never dreamed that lifting weights could help women achieve the toned and lean bodies they desired. But the correct amount of repetitions and resistance can totally transform a woman's body in a very short amount of time. It's exciting!

Of course, it's not easy. Resistance training is tough. I've been known to grunt and moan and make faces in the weight room myself. It's hard work! Jeff, my husband, and I embarked on the Body for Life program three years ago. We felt really good at the end of those twelve weeks, and we looked a lot better, too! But those twelve weeks of disciplined workouts and a restricted eating program sure were difficult to get through. There were days when I dreaded getting out of bed in the morning because I knew my calves would ache the minute my feet hit the floor. Yep, we worked hard and saw results!

Resistance, whether in the natural or the spiritual realm, is never much fun, but it always produces change. During those stormy times in life—the times when you're in the valley and you're wondering if you'll ever see a mountaintop again—that's when the real growth occurs. That's when you become stretched. That's when you find out what you're made of. When you're going through the fire, that's when all of the chaff is burned away, leaving a beautiful, better version of you. So if you're going through some sort of resistance in life right now, don't fight it! Like James says, count it all joy! You're one step closer to revealing a new and improved you!

"HOPELESSLY DEVOTED"

Near the cross of Jesus stood his mother,
his mother's sister, Mary the wife of Clopas,
and Mary Magdalene.
JOHN 19:25 NIV

I grew up watching *Grease*, starring John Travolta and Olivia Newton John. My favorite scene? I love it when Olivia Newton John walks around the baby pool in the backyard in her nightgown singing "Hopelessly Devoted to You." (You're singing along right now, aren't you?) Of course, in that scene, she is singing of her character's devotion to John Travolta's character—her summer love.

One source on Dictionary.com includes "commitment to some purpose" and "religious zeal; willingness to serve God" in its definition of devotion. But we can be devoted to many things—our beauty routines, our workout schedules, our diet plans, our husbands, our families, our churches, and so on.

Devotion can be a very noble character trait. You see glimpses of devotion throughout the Bible—especially in the story of the Cross. Jesus was devoted to the Father—so much so that He was willing to die a horrible death to fulfill God's salvation plan so that we could spend eternity with Him. And though some of Jesus' followers dissociated themselves from Jesus for fear of being crucified, too, the women didn't disown Him. It tells us in John 19:25 that Mary, the mother of

Jesus; Jesus' aunt; Mary the wife of Clopas; and Mary Magdalene stayed at the foot of the cross, even though they were implicating themselves just by being there. They were devoted to Him. They loved Him more than they loved themselves. They were willing to stay with Him until the very end.

That is the kind of devotion that makes a difference in your life and in the lives of others. Let me ask you today: What are you truly devoted to? Your job? Your family? Your money? Are you so devoted to your workout routine that you give it priority over your morning devotional time? Or are you willing to spend time at the foot of the Cross, just basking in His presence? That's what devotion is all about. You know what's so amazing about Jesus? The Word says if you seek Him, all of the other things will be added to you. It's a win-win situation!

Unlike the song's lyrics, you won't be "Hope-lessly Devoted" when devoting your life to Jesus. Once you pledge your love and life to Jesus, you'll become "Hopeful and Devoted to Him." Jesus is all about hope. Your destiny lies in your devotion to Him. So go ahead and pledge your devotion to Jesus today. If you do, your life is guaranteed to be beautiful!

FROM AN UGLY DUCKLING TO A BEAUTIFUL SWAN

"I will give you a new heart with new and right desires, and I will put a new spirit in you. I will take out your stony heart of sin and give you a new, obedient heart."

EZEKIEL 36:26 NLT

Have you ever seen the reality show on Fox called *The Swan*? It's amazing. The show selects plain-Jane women and some really homely gals, too, and through plastic surgery, cosmetic dentistry, lots of liposuction, personal training and diet modifications, hair color and extensions, microderm abrasion, and sometimes other minor surgeries, these women come out looking like supermodels. Then, at the end of the show, the finalists compete for "The Swan" beauty queen crown. Pretty wild, isn't it?

I watched the show in amazement the first two seasons, all the while deciding what I would ask to have altered, sucked, and tucked should I ever get the chance to be on a show like that. (I bet you did the same thing if you watched!) What was most interesting to me was when the "new and improved" women met with their families for the first time after their dramatic transformations. Sometimes the women looked so different, their babies didn't even know them! And their husbands couldn't stop staring at them. Talk about a makeover! These women weren't even recognizable. From their teeth to their toenails, they were totally improved in every way. Though there was some pain and suffering involved over their three-month transformation, the end result was beautifully astonishing.

Well, we may not be able to be featured on any television makeover shows, but we can have that same sort of life-altering makeover on the inside simply by letting the Master do His best work. The minute we receive Jesus as our Lord and Savior, He wipes the slate clean and gives us a new start. The Word says we actually become new creatures.

And that's not all! After our initial God experience, He continues making minor adjustments in our attitudes, and before long, we're hardly the same person. Our likes and dislikes change. The places we want to hang out change. The way we choose to take care of our bodies (the temple of the Holy Spirit) changes. Even our friend choices change. And over time, we leave that old, ugly duckling spirit behind and emerge a beautiful swan.

When you get a makeover by the Master, you will become more confident in who you are, and people will automatically be drawn to you. When you spend time with the Lord, you're like a people magnet. They won't know why they like you—they just will! You become more attractive.

You smile more. You laugh more. You love more. Why not let the Master give you a makeover today? There's a beautiful swan in you just waiting to escape.

SIMPLY IRRESISTIBLE

Love never fails.
1 CORINTHIANS 13:8 NIV

If you found out you could become simply irresistible, wouldn't you want to know how? If the ability to become irresistible came in a bottle, wouldn't you rush to the store to buy it? You probably would, because people from all walks of life would love to know that secret. Women pay millions of dollars every year on beauty products and cosmetic surgery to look better. Women spend millions per year on the weight-loss and exercise industry in order to lose extra pounds and attain better physiques. And women invest loads of money in designer clothing, shoes, and accessories to improve their images. It seems we'd all like to be irresistible.

The advertising executives know this, which is why they call perfumes "Very Irresistible" and other similar names. These advertising executives know women desire that irresistible quality and that they'll pay almost anything to achieve it.

Well, search no more. I have the secret to being irresistible, and you can't get it in a bottle or a potion of any kind. You can't buy it. You can't even get it by working out at a gym. You'll only find it in the Bible. God's love is what makes us irresistible. The more you have on the inside of you, the more irresistible you'll become.

See, people are drawn to the love of God. They long for it. God made us that way—with a void inside that can only be filled and satisfied with His love. Here's some additional good news: God's love never fails. The devil has no weapon that can stand up against the love of God. It makes you irresistible, but it also enables you to resist the devil and his evil attacks. Open God's Word and read 1 Corinthians 13 today, and ask the Lord to fill you with His love. Soon, you'll be absolutely irresistible.

Other books by
MICHELLE MEDLOCK ADAMS

Daily Wisdom for Mothers

Especially for women with children at home, this book offers a year's worth of brief, relevant, biblical reflections with monthly themes such as worry, unconditional love, discipline, and prayer.

ISBN 1-59310-175-9 / 384 pages / $5.97

Daily Wisdom for Working Women
(with Gena Maselli)

Packed with motivation, encouragement, and humor, this 365-day devotional is targeted toward working women ages 25–45. It tackles issues like competition, identity, emotions, contentment, and office politics.

ISBN 1-59310-426-X / 384 pages / $5.97

Available wherever Christian books are sold.

If you enjoyed

(SECRETS OF)

B&AUTY

be sure to check out Rebecca Barlow Jordan's
title. . .also available from Barbour Publishing:

DAILY
IN YOUR
IMAGE

ISBN 1-59310-157-0

Available wherever Christian books are sold.